Great Western Road Vehicles

DOMINE · DIRIGE · NOS

VIRTUTE · ET · INDUSTRIA

Great Western
Road Vehicles

Philip J. Kelley

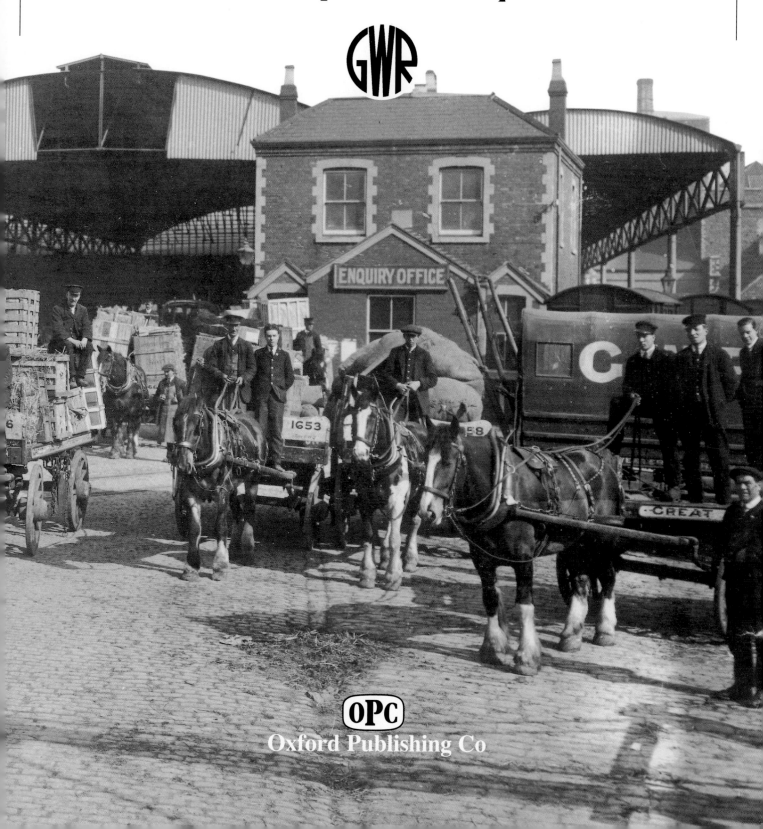

OPC
Oxford Publishing Co

Acknowledgements

When I wrote the two original volumes concerning the road vehicles of the Great Western Railway I very much appreciated the help given to me by many people. Once again I would like to thank the following retired British Rail staff for their assistance: Keith Montague and Neil Sprinks, former PRO, Paddington; W. R. MacDonald, CCE, Paddington; C. Chilvers and C. Froud, Swindon; Ian Coulson, Records Office, Royal Oak; and Robert Verner-Jeffreys, Road Motor Engineer BR(W).

Other people who have been very helpful are Frank Dumbleton, David Hyde, John Edgington, Bernard Harding, Keith Steele and Stan Dickson. I would particularly like to thank John Cummings for his untiring assistance throughout.

I would like to mention others who are sadly no longer with us: Jim Russell, Mike Ogden and G. W. Dascombe (former Thornycroft Archivist), and Peter Thatcher.

I would also like to thank my fellow Trustees of the Great Western Trust at Didcot for their considerable help and loan of records and photographs.

Finally my sincerest thanks go to my wife Dorothy for all her understanding and encouragement during my work on this and my previous books.

Philip J. Kelley
2002

Title page: **Bristol Temple Meads Goods Depot on 12 March 1924, where the photographer has brought the whole place to a standstill! A 3¹/₂-ton AEC takes the spotlight, while there are also various types of single-horse-drawn wagons, one with a black tilt. This photograph gives a very good idea of the amount of cartage traffic in the 1920s.**

Left: **A Thornycroft 4-ton chassis fitted with a flat body, Fleet No B733, is seen at Wexcombe Manor, Marlborough on 30 September 1937, undertaking household removal. (See also page 123 on household removal.)** *BR*

Readers will appreciate the valuable and historic nature of a number of images reproduced within this book. As it has not been possible to obtain the originals, recourse has been made to the use of photographs and photocopies for reproduction purposes.

First published 2002

ISBN 0 86093 568 X

Published by Oxford Publishing Co

an imprint of Ian Allan Publishing Ltd, Hersham, Surrey KT12 4RG.

Printed by Ian Allan Printing Ltd, Hersham, Surrey KT12 4RG.

Code 0207/A3

The majority of the photographs in this volume are from the Great Western Trust at Didcot, while a number are from the author's collection The illustration on page 32 is from the R. S. Carpenter collection, and those on page 75 are from AEC.

Contents

Introduction 7

1. Horse-drawn Goods Vehicles 9

2. Horse-drawn Passenger Vehicles 29

3. Mechanical Cartage Vehicles 33

4. The Country Lorry Services 63

5. Railhead Services 107

6. The Zonal Goods Organisation 138

7. Mechanical Horses, Tractors and Trailers 143

8. Motor Omnibuses 177

9. Miscellaneous Vehicles 221

Appendix I. 'Motor Car' Service Statistics 231

Appendix II. Payments to Drivers 231

Appendix III. Official Drawings of GWR Horse-drawn Vehicles 232

Above: The old and the new: road vehicles at Paddington on 9 September 1943 showing, from left to right, a 6-ton Scammell three-wheel tractor and trailer, pair-horse wagon No 619 with Carter Smith in the chair, and a Bedford four-wheel tractor and trailer, Fleet No S8812.

Above: **1930 Dennis flat platform lorry No B2341 demonstrates the GWR's house removal service. Showing the standard K type furniture container.**

Left: **Bristol Temple Meads, showing the station forecourt and below two Thornycroft vehicles with van bodies and a Scammell mechanical horse and trailer, all on joint GWR and LMS services.** *Author's collection*

Introduction

Twenty-eight years ago my first book on *Road Vehicles of the Great Western Railway* was published, followed by the Appendix in 1982. Since then more information, photographs and drawings have come to light, some from retired Great Western Road Motor staff. It has therefore been decided to republish both books as one volume, retaining much of the original and incorporating many additions.

This album is not intended to be a concise history. Personally, I think that would be impossible as so much of the official records have been lost or destroyed. I have tried to be as accurate as possible, but much detail is subject to conjecture.

The drawings include direct copies of official diagrams; some have been supplied by vehicle manufacturers and others have been specially drawn by Stan Dickson and the late Peter Thatcher. The book has been compiled, as before, under four main headings: horse-drawn vehicles; mechanically propelled cartage vehicles; motor omnibuses (Road Motors); and miscellaneous vehicles. There is an introduction to each section.

As regards livery, most of the GWR's road vehicles followed very closely that of rail passenger coaches, being either chocolate brown and cream, all-over chocolate brown, or crimson lake,

according to the period. Some early omnibuses had plain varnished bodies similar to GER/LNER teak, and a few were thought to have been green, as were the Foden steam wagons. Lettering consisted of the full 'Great Western Railway' or just the initials 'GWR', either in gold leaf or cream, and with or without shading. Sometimes the lettering was cast iron similar to signalbox nameboards. The coat of arms was rarely used. The canvas tilt, or hood, where fitted, was either black or cream with the appropriate white or black lettering; on some vehicles brown lettering appeared on cream tilts. Quite often a panel was provided for the provision of a poster. There were many variations and exceptions to the foregoing.

Horses were of course used from the very beginning, and later worked side by side with their mechanical brothers right up to nationalisation and beyond. The GWR was undoubtedly one of the pioneers in the use of mechanically propelled road vehicles, first for cartage in 1902 and for passengers in 1903. Many experimental units were tried using different methods of propulsion. The mechanical horse and trailer were the final stage of that development before the Great Western Railway went out of existence in 1947.

Above: **A photograph showing the Thornycroft 30cwt and 4-ton chassis vehicles supplied to the GWR. See also pages 90 and 92.** *Author's collection*

A good view of the Paddington area with the goods depot on the left and the canal on the right. The photographs was taken on 14 August 1925 to depict the shunting horse as opposed to the delivery horse. *BR*

Chapter One:
Horse-drawn Goods Vehicles

The introduction of steam traction led people to suppose that the services of the railway horse would be rendered unnecessary, or at any rate greatly restricted, but this was not so, and in 1909 the Great Western Railway still had more than 3,000 horses. By 31 December 1926 the actual number on stud was 2,828, compared with 2,896 in the previous year. In 1936 the number was down to 2,000, and by the end of the year it was 1,773, of which 500 were employed in London. The arrival of the mechanical horse and trailer in the 1930s had its desired effect in reducing the numbers of horses on strength; just after World War 2 the total was 1,000, and they finally disappeared in places like Evesham in 1952 and Paddington in 1954. The horse served the Great Western Railway well, despite the increasing use of motor vehicles.

The average price paid for a horse in 1926 was £44. The GWR purchased them when they were five to six years of age and they were good for anything from 6 to 12 years on cartage services. The majority came from North and Central Wales where a suitable type was bred. When a batch was purchased each animal was harnessed to a pair-horse van in company with an experienced horse, and much care was taken in allocating horses to a class of work suitable to their strength and mobility.

The GWR maintained a very large Provender Store at Didcot, now demolished. The Directors of the Company insisted that all the provender should be grown in English soil. The weekly consumption averaged 1,000 sacks of oats, 220 sack of beans, 480 sacks of maize, 110 tons of hay, 16 tons of oat straw and 18 tons of bran, while for bedding 40 to 50 tons of straw were used. The approximate cost per annum was £70,000. Apparently, London horses had less oats and hay than the country horses and their daily allowance of provender varied from 27lb to 32lb.

There were few street accidents causing injury to horses, which spoke well of the judgement of the drivers, especially in later days with the advent of the motor vehicle. Most drivers served their apprenticeship as van guards, and, after training, were advanced to chain-horse drivers, then by successive stages to carmen with one horse, then pair-horse, three-horse and four-horse teams. Drivers were instructed to provide against starting hurriedly or pulling up quickly. Every effort was to be made to keep horses cool and they were not allowed to make their own pace, being kept at walking pace both up and down hills. At no time were they permitted to drink from public water troughs; a bucket was carried on every vehicle and the water collected from a pure source.

The livery of horse-drawn vehicles varied considerably, but at one time horse road vans used for delivering goods traffic had red wheels, shafts and framing, and those used for collecting and delivering passenger train parcels were painted chocolate all over. In 1909 the latter vehicles also were given red shafts and wheels.

Below: '**How NOT to Skid the Wheel**' and '**The SAFE Way**': an extract from the *Great Western Railway Magazine* of May 1915, part of a campaign to draw attention to safe working.

Above: Single-horse-drawn light spring cart No 1288, built at Swindon Works and photographed in 1890. The company initials and number are stamped on the shaft.

Below: Single-horse parcels van No 143, also built at Swindon Works and photographed in 1890.

Above: Single-horse wagon No 2401. The tare weight is shown as '1-1-3' (1ton 1cwt 3qr). Built at Swindon Works and seen in January 1900, it is fitted with a foot-brake, while the chain apparatus hanging on the side is a skid for placing under the rear wheel when the vehicle is stationary. Note the luxury seating arrangement, complete with a facility for holding the whip. Most horse-drawn vehicles were allocated to a particular station and were branded accordingly.

Below: This is single-horse wagon No 100, with a tare weight of less than 1 ton. Built at Swindon Works and photographed on 11 January 1905, it is also fitted with a foot-brake, and is of a very similar design to vehicle No 2401, with minor differences. The plate on the side states that the load is not to exceed 2 tons; this was quite a load for one horse, as the official recognised load, in the London area, for a powerful horse was 30-35cwt, or 3t 10cwt for a pair.

Above: Swindon-built single-horse passenger train parcels van No 231 has a tare weight of 0-14-2. Photographed in February 1900, it is again fitted with a foot-brake, with 'GWR' stamped on the brass wheel bosses and the inside of the felloes (wheel rims). This vehicle was based and maintained at Bristol.

Below: Van No 232 has a tare weight of 0-14-0 (written on the negative but not on the vehicle) and is almost identical to No 231.

Scale 7mm/1ft

© R.T.HATCHER. 1972.

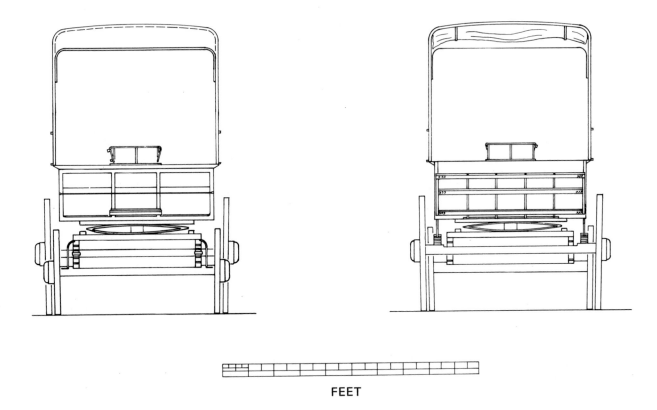

FEET

Above: **Scale drawing of a single-horse passenger train parcels van.**

Above: Single-horse parcels van No 243, with a tare weight of 0-7-3, was used for deliveries in the Henley-on-Thames area. Built at Swindon Works and photographed in February 1900, it was fitted with a hand-brake and, as with most Swindon productions, had 'GWR' stamped on the brass wheel bosses.

Below left: Pair-horse passenger train parcels delivery van No 166 P, with a tare weight of 1-1-0. Again Swindon-built, and photographed in May 1902, this vehicle is fitted with a foot-brake. Underneath the van, resting on the axles, is the perch to which the two horses were attached when in its normal position.

Below right: This single-horse express parcel van, No 305, was built at Swindon Works and photographed on 6 May 1908. It was also fitted with a foot-brake. Note the windows in the side of the tilt. The turning circle does not appear to be very great.

Above: **Photographed on 5 April 1909 is single-horse lorry No 1422, built at Swindon Works and fitted with a foot-brake. Note the heavier construction of this vehicle, with thicker spokes and felloes. The plate on the front shows that the load is not to exceed 2 tons, for a tare of 0-18-3.**

Left: **Foot-brake-fitted single-horse parcels collecting van No 287 was built at Swindon Works and photographed on 14 August 1909. The amount of lettering on the tilt is unbelievable, with many typefaces in use – a modeller's nightmare! This van would start its day from Paddington loaded with parcels for delivery, then for the rest of day it would be based at the Strand Office for collections.**

15

Above: This three-horse team is harnessed to wagon No 532, built at Swindon Works and photographed in 1909. It was basically designed to be hauled by two horses, but when required, due to hilly conditions or heavy loads, an additional horse (a chain horse) was attached. Hoops and tarpaulin are fitted, as is a foot-brake, fully applied. Note the carter's apron.

Below: Here a four-horse team is seen in 1909 with Swindon-built wagon No 546. This vehicle was fitted with two single-horse shafts and obviously additional chain horses were needed because of the load. One hopes that the goods have been loaded systematically and that the first item to be delivered is not at the bottom! Notice that the carter has a plank as a seat, unlike in the previous picture. The vehicle is fitted with a screw-type brake worked from the side of the lorry.

Above: An expensive shipment by any standards! The two wagons are each drawn by four-horse teams, two in the shafts and two chain horses. This load, circa 1909, is cases of Dunville & Co's whisky. Notice that the wagons have no seats for the carmen.

Below: A very crowded and busy scene at Paddington Goods Yard around 1909. Most of the vehicles are two- or four-horse wagons, some fitted with hoops for tarpaulins. Some are also fitted with seats for the carmen; as already mentioned, where no seats were fitted the carmen sat on planks, or even on the edge of the wagon itself. Note that the loading, in some cases, appears to be very precarious.

Above: **Pair-horse wagon No 408 was built at Swindon Works, with a tare of 1-14-2. Photographed around 1914, it is complete with a foot-brake, and instead of the usual canvas tilt it has a heavy timber type.**

Below: **Pair-horse lorry No 1223, used for conveying boilers, was photographed at Swindon Works in November 1903. It was a very robust vehicle with solid metal wheels; extra chain horses could be provided when necessary. The tare weight of this vehicle, with skids, was 6-4-0.**

This pair-horse plate-glass float is being used to convey a 4½-ton bronze statue of General Sir Redvers Buller from the works at Thames Ditton to Brentford Goods for onward transmission by train to Exeter. The cast plate near the rear of the vehicle shows that any load must not exceed 7 tons.

Many pictures have been published showing special trains loaded with blankets at Witney. This 1912 photograph shows them after being offloaded from the railway at Paddington Goods Yard, and ready to depart, in convoy, for Maple's in London. The wagons are all of the same type with loads not to exceed 4t 10cwt.

Above: A standard pair-horse wagon, No 2136, fitted with a foot-brake and thought to be at Poplar, circa 1914. The tare weight is about 1-1-0 and the cast plate shows that the load is not to exceed 4t 10cwt. The wagon came out of Swindon Works on 20 January 1911.

Below: Pair-horse lorry No 3536, tare 1-7-3, is fitted with a seat and foot-brake, and is shown here loaded with a container that was probably used for carrying slates. The photograph was taken circa 1930.

Above: A single-horse steel-tyred Timber Float, tare 1-4-0, photographed at Hockley on 28 October 1935.

Below: Pair-horse delivery wagon No 535 was built at Swindon Works and photographed at Paddington in May 1937, fitted with hoops, tarpaulin and a foot-brake, which is fully applied. Carter Smith is in the chair again (see page 5); note his fancy whip handle complete with bow. The chain between the wheels is used for locking the rear wheels when stationary. The advertisement is very interesting – cigarettes were 10 for fourpence (2p).

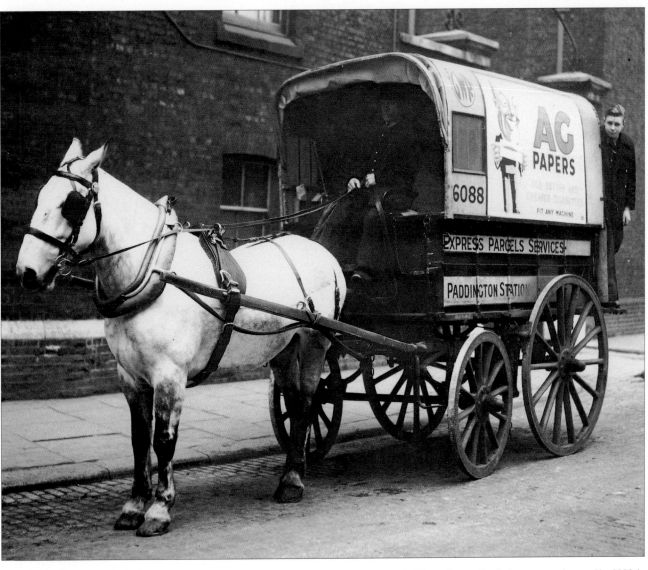

Above: Single-horse parcels van No 6088 is seen near Mint Stables, Paddington, in or about 1936. It is of interest that the tilt is painted cream, when they were usually black. The van also bears the 1934 monogram. Notice the very lightweight wheels.

Left: Single-horse wagon No 2699 complete with hoops and tarpaulin; notice the very elaborate carved back to the carman's seat. Behind is a 30cwt forward-control Burford chassis with a platform body, also complete with hoops and tarpaulin. The photograph was taken at Paddington Goods on 15 February 1930 outside the GWR Fire Station.

Above: Pair-horse lorries Nos 1083 and 1080 are leaving Westbourne Park Goods Yard in April 1939 with a load of Anderson shelter parts. Just prior to the war this was an urgent exercise and every available mode of road transport was used to carry out this distribution (see also page 156). Britain was not prepared for much that happened in World War 2, but air raid shelters got away to an early start.

Below: Single-horse lorry No 4081 was built Swindon Works. Photographed on 9 July 1941, it is fitted with a foot-brake, but is not complete, as no seat is fitted. The tare is 0-17-0, and the load is not to exceed 2 tons. Note that the edges of the shafts and the wheel bosses have been painted white to facilitate visibility in the blackout during World War 2. A vehicle of this type has just been restored and is on show at Steam: Museum of the GWR at Swindon.

Above: Single-horse parcels van No 4901, was photographed on 3 October 1937, and represented the ultimate in horse-drawn vehicle design. Experimentally introduced in Oxford, it had several modern features, including ball-bearing axleboxes, pneumatic tyres and electric lighting. Hub brakes were also installed, similar to motor car practice, instead of a primitive shoe working on the exterior of an iron tyre. The driver's seat was recessed and protected from the weather by a projecting canopy and a scuttle dash at the front.

Below: Standing in a square near Paddington station in April 1938 is single-horse parcels van No 4902. Parcel carter Mr T. Hoare won first prize with this turn-out in the London van horse parade in Regent's Park on Easter Monday 1938. He also received the RSPCA medal for the best undocked horse in the parade.

Above: A GWR '9hp' team is moving a 17½-ton Burrell Showman's engine from the Agricultural Hall to Paddington for conveyance to Plymouth on 30 January 1922. This Showman's engine was built by Charles Burrell & Sons Ltd in 1922, works No 3912, and was an 8nhp DCC machine built for Anderton & Rowland. It has since been preserved by a Mr W. G. Chamberlain of Peterborough and the sides rewritten with 'Pride of the Fens'.

Below: This is the Road Wagon Shop (Wheel Section) of Swindon Works on 16 January 1915, which was built on the site of the original wagon shop. At that time there were upwards of 3,600 horse-drawn road vehicles in use, so the importance of such a depot can be realised. The GWR adopted the 'Artillery'-pattern wheel because of its strength, and it proved ideal. This type of wheel had extra spokes and was developed by the Army; should one or two spokes be shot away during battle conditions the wheel would still remain sound. The shop turned out as many as 300 wheels a week.

Above: A view of Swindon Works' Road Wagon Shop on 31 July 1907.

Left: Another 16 January 1915 photograph of the Road Wagon Shop. This was the heyday of the horse-drawn vehicle, as the mechanically propelled type was only just making itself felt.

Left: Wheels within wheels! Discarded wagon wheels are stacked outside the GWR's Alfred Road Garage at Westbourne Park, West London, on 10 July 1934.

Above: Flash photography helps illuminate this dingy gas-lit view of the large Farriers Shop in the Mint Stables near Paddington on 16 March 1936. In a report written in 1937, it was stated that 1,700 horses were owned by the company and that 500 were employed in London, most of them at Paddington. In order to cater for this number the stabling was centralised in a large three-storey building at South Wharf Road, known as Mint Stables. Apart from the stabling and Farriers Shop, there was also a laundry where horses' collars were cleaned and dried! Horseshoes were made here and fitted; some horses, like humans, had an uneven tread and had a new pair of shoes every fortnight, although a month was the normal interval. Shoeing was a swift business, and it used to take about an hour to completely reshoe a horse.

Below: The Horse Hospital at West Ealing, seen here in 1909, adjoined the Great Western Athletic Ground. In the winter 24 horses could be tended in stables, while in summer 40 could be dealt with. Note the two-wheeled water carrier in the foreground, built at Swindon – not all tenders were metal!

Chapter 2:
Horse-drawn Passenger Vehicles

Prior to August 1903, and even after that date, the Great Western Railway used horse-drawn passenger vehicles to connect with trains. They were, of course, also used by contractors and railway staff when surveying the line prior to and during construction. Apparently Brunel decided that he should have his own personal horse-drawn carriage, and therefore designed and had built the famous 'Britska', which was nicknamed the 'Flying Hearse',

mainly because it was painted black. It was designed to hold his plans and instruments, together with his notable cigars. The seating was so arranged that it could be adapted when required for Brunel to sleep on board. Quite a feat if travelling on rough roads! The vehicle had no windows, just ventilators.

The following illustrations show some examples of these carriages, which were preserved for a period of time.

Above: **Brunel's 'Britska'.**

Below left: **Contemporary reports and official Swindon photographic records state that this two-horse or four-horse coach, named** *Galloper,* **is the vehicle that Brunel designed and had built when he wished to be accompanied by directors and other officials. The photograph was taken in 1894 at Swindon, and shows the carriage apparently in a very special livery.**

Below right: **The building date of this single-horse omnibus is not known, but it was photographed at Swindon Works in May 1894. It is fitted with a foot-brake, and a very simple garter surrounding two crests adorns the side below the lettering.**

Above: A pair-horse or four-horse omnibus of circa 1889, bearing a paint date of 9 April 1906, is seen here at Westbourne Park. It is fitted with outside passenger seats and the roof is adapted for luggage. It is understood that this vehicle was stored for a period, possibly for preservation. Notice the octagonal rim to the front nave (hub), probably the first foothold for the postilion to reach the driving seat. The robust hand-brake is very noticeable.

Below: This pair-horse or four-horse saloon omnibus, also seen at Westbourne Park, caters for inside passengers only, and is another example of a vehicle stored for possible preservation. This could be the same type of vehicle as shown in the lower left photograph on the previous page, but is less decorative except for the garter and crest on the side. Note the ventilation grilles behind the postilion's footboard.

Above: A four-horse omnibus, also kept for possible preservation, is seen again at Westbourne Park. The rear staircase is for outside passengers, probably fourth class! The vehicle is fitted with a centrally positioned hand-brake, which looks to be a much better, and more practical, system working on both back wheels. The livery in this case is more like the Great Western's usual standard.

Below: A drawing of a four-horse omnibus, dated February 1889, which may be compared with the photograph above.

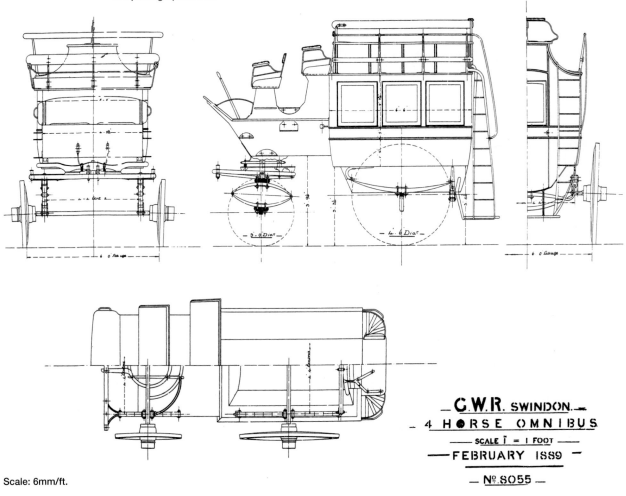

Scale: 6mm/ft.

G.W.R. SWINDON.
4 HORSE OMNIBUS
SCALE 1 = 1 FOOT
FEBRUARY 1889
Nº SO55

Above: A four-horse omnibus or 'stagecoach', shown here outside the Southern National Omnibus Company's premises in Lee Road, Lynton, Devon, in August 1935. The vehicle originally belonged to a Mr Tom Jones of Lynton, who ran the Lynton to Minehead road service that connected with Great Western Railway trains until 1920. It would be interesting to know what the livery was behind the entwined GWR initials. The photograph, taken by Hubert Wheeler, was kindly supplied by Roger Carpenter.

Chapter 3:
Mechanical Cartage Vehicles

The Great Western Railway first entered the mechanical commercial vehicle era in 1902 with a steam wagon supplied by the Thornycroft Steam Wagon Company Ltd. Following the success enjoyed by Thornycroft with the War Office in supplying steam wagons for the South African war, Mr F. C. A. Coventry, Assistant to the Carriage Works Manager at Swindon and responsible for Road Motor work, visited the firm in May 1902 to investigate the use of a similar type for railway cartage work. Shortly afterwards a vehicle was put into service at Hockley, Birmingham, where it was on trial for several months. The success of the trial convinced the GWR that mechanical traction was definitely the answer for cartage work.

After the initial steam wagon there followed two Milnes-Daimler lorries and two Wallis Stevens steam tractors in 1904/5. Other types were added, and, according to an official GWR report of 1909, the goods and parcel service was operated by the following mechanically propelled vehicles supporting the horse-drawn type:

Birkenhead	1 steam wagon, 3 motor parcel vans
Paddington Goods	2 petrol lorries, 2 electric vehicles
Bilston Goods	2 steam traction engines
Slough Goods	1 petrol lorry
Saltash & Callington	1 petrol lorry
Cardiff	2 motor parcel vans
Birmingham	3 motor parcel vans

Above: A drawing of a standard undertype 4-ton steam wagon, as manufactured by the Thornycroft Steam Wagon Company Ltd in 1903.

Below: This photograph shows a Thornycroft undertype steam wagon which was supplied, on trial, to the Lancashire & Yorkshire Railway. A similar vehicle to this was supplied to the GWR in 1902, also on trial. See drawing above.

An experimental electric vehicle was introduced in 1906 and another type was built at Slough in 1908.

In 1910 a total of 25 mechanical cartage vehicles were in service. The Straker Squire 12hp vans, added in 1909, were built to the design and specification of the Great Western Railway. In 1914 the bulk orders from John I. Thornycroft & Co Ltd commenced.

World War 1 encouraged the use of mechanical transport and in 1919 surplus Army vehicles were dumped at Slough Trading Estate. The Great Western purchased 130 AEC 3½-ton lorries from this collection, which were somewhat reconstructed with interchangeable bodies in order that they could serve as charabancs in summer and as goods vehicles in winter. Further electric vehicles of a different type entered service in 1919.

In 1924 the GWR inaugurated contract hire by which vans were allotted for the exclusive use of any companies that required them, and were painted in their own liveries. On 4 January 1926 Macfarlane, Lang & Co entered into such a contract with the GWR.

Owing to the enormous increase in the numbers of road vehicles used by the GWR, more accommodation for their repair became necessary, and the Road Transport Department at Slough, originally set up in 1905, built a new brick structure in 1926.

Many vehicles of special types were introduced to cater for very diverse forms of traffic, such as the large 10-ton six-wheeled Thornycroft for sand and gravel cartage at Theale. As with the majority of vehicles, the chassis were purchased from the manufacturer and the bodies were built by the GWR

During 1929 the total of vehicles was increased by 287 units, including examples of the AEC 4/5 ton, Thornycroft 30cwt, High Capacity stock supplied by Foden, Thornycroft and Scammell (some fitted with tipping bodies), Harvester and Fordson tractors, and additional Carrimore and Eagle trailers. Foden steam wagons were purchased in 1929 for heavy cartage work.

In 1930 the progress of cartage work continued unchecked: goods tonnage increased by 200,000 tons and there were 1,200,000 more parcels carried. This led to the authorisation of 152 new vehicles comprising 30 of 6 to 8 tons, 100 of 1½ to 2 tons, and 22 tractors and trailers. The year 1931 brought the total of vehicles to 1,486, a further 148 new vehicles having been added.

September 1931 saw the introduction of the now familiar articulated vehicles (apart from an experimental type in 1918). These virtually sounded the death-knell of the horse-drawn types,

and by January 1937 there were 333 3-ton three-wheelers, 194 6-ton three-wheelers and 49 6-ton four-wheelers.

During 1932 a number of special vehicles were purchased, including lorries with movable floors, a number of 'Farmers'-type vehicles, specially constructed livestock lorries, and 15 container trailers. More specialised vehicles and trailers were purchased in 1933, in order to accommodate almost every conceivable type of traffic carried on the railway.

In 1934 £150,000 was spent on about 350 vehicles and trailers, about 100 of which were renewals. In 1935 £80,000 was authorised to be spent on new vehicles, together with a further £60,000 for renewals.

The Great Western Railway's authorised cartage equipment on 31 December 1936 comprised 2,328 mechanised units, 1,589 trailers and 1,773 horses. The consumption of petrol in the same year was approximately 2,177,500 gallons.

In January 1936 Mr Charles Willis, the first Great Western Motor Lorry Driver, retired. It is interesting to note that, about this time, the Great Western carried out experiments with a tachograph in the cabs of some lorries. In July 1936 the Directors authorised additional vehicles costing £75,405, and a further £44,765 for renewals. At the end of 1936 the totals of authorised cartage equipment were 2,328 mechanical units, 1,589 trailers and 1,773 horses. The numbers of articulated vehicles at the end of that year were 333 3-ton three-wheelers, 194 6-ton three-wheelers, and 49 6-ton four-wheelers, and the consumption of petrol during 1936 was 2,177,500 gallons.

At the end of 1937 the authorised cartage equipment was 2,431 GWR-owned and 21 jointly owned, with 1,845 GWR trailers and 12 jointly owned. In that year £67,990 was authorised for 124 new vehicles and 50 trailers, with £41,640 being allocated for renewals, and £4,525 for improvements.

The world situation in 1938 had its effect and only renewals were authorised on 103 cartage vehicles and 14 trailers. A further £2,500 was made available for the conversion of solid-tyred trailers to pneumatic tyres, rendered necessary by new legislation. The authorised stock on 31 December 1938 was 2,393 GWR vehicles and 23 jointly owned, with 1,865 GWR trailers and 12 jointly owned.

The London Parcels Cartage Service based at Paddington in 1938 consisted of 96 motors, varying in capacity from 1 to 8 tons. The total normal mileage was 3,400 miles daily, 132 regular rounds being operated, of which 123 were by motor and the remainder by horse. A good average day's traffic was 37,000 parcels. In 1930 the cartage staff numbered 112 and the number of parcels dealt with was 6,873,000. In 1938 there were 136 vanmen and 10,170,000 parcels. Figures like these give some idea of the size of the company's fleet.

A certain amount of Parliamentary legislation affected the running of the road motor fleet in the 1930s, such as the Road Traffic Act 1930, which had important provisions regarding hours of staff, vehicle weights, speed and third party insurance. The Road and Rail Traffic Act 1933 embodied a scheme for licensing commercial road vehicles: (1) Public Carriers Licence 'A', (2) Limited Carriers Licence 'B', and (3) Private Carriers Licence 'C'. The Finance Act 1933 entirely reorganised the scale of taxation for motor vehicles, which added about £30,000 a year to the GWR's road vehicle expenses. Alterations were necessary in the way of lightening vehicles to bring them within the lower category for licensing, by replacing solid rubber tyres with pneumatic and disposing of trailers not fitted with rubber tyres.

During 1936 it became necessary for any person who was not in the possession of a driver's licence before 1 April 1934 to take a test. A further condition demanded that those drivers who handled certain types classified as heavy goods vehicles, and who had not driven such vehicles for a qualifying period, had to be examined.

Lorry Makes and Types, Cartage Motors, 1925-8

		1925	1926	1927	1928
Straker Squire	1 ton	12	3	2	–
Thornycroft	30cwt	31	46	72	117
AEC	3½ ton	303	303	342	361
Burford	30cwt	135	135	135	147
Ford	1 ton	21	21	40	38
Traffic	2 ton	1	1	1	1
Commer	3 ton	1	1	1	1
Burford	15cwt	6	6	6	6
Maudslay	5 ton	1	1	–	–
Milnes-Daimler	5 ton	2	2	–	–
Fordson tractors		16	25	42	42
Knox tractor		1	1	1	1
Electrics		7	3	–	–
Thornycroft	3½ ton	–	1	2	2
Thornycroft	4/5 ton	–	50	57	106
Carette		–	6	6	6
Maudslay	3 ton	–	5	5	–
Harvester tractor		–	1	1	1
Morris	1 ton	–	–	3	26
Bean		–	–	1	1
Scammell six-wheeler		–	–	1	1
Daimler	3 ton	–	–	3	3
Ford	7cwt	1	1	1	1
S & D Freighter		–	–	–	1

Employers of more than 250 drivers of mechanically propelled vehicles could appoint their own examiners, so a new school for this purpose was established at Taplow in 1939.

As from 1 January 1937 it became compulsory for all windscreens to consist of safety glass, while speedometers became compulsory on vehicles placed in service on and after 1 October 1937. Special plates were to be carried from that date by vehicles limited to a legal speed of 20mph and by trailers.

The principal effort in the Road Transport Department during 1939 was directed to Government work. An additional 25 vehicles and 50 trailers were acquired, and 182 condemned motor vehicles and 10 trailers were replaced. The authorised company stock on 31 December 1939 was 2,450 GWR-owned and 23 jointly owned, with 2,164 GWR trailers and 12 jointly owned. There was a need for economy in the use of petrol because of the war, which necessitated an expansion of the horse stud to 1,600!

The following pages and photographs will tell more conclusively the story of the Great Western's enterprise in the road cartage business.

On a number of these photographs the original fleet numbers have been altered in ink to show the new numbers to be allocated under a later renumbering scheme.

Above: Milnes-Daimler 20hp goods lorry No A-7645, one of the type introduced in 1904. Notice the simple steel chassis with horse-drawn-vehicle-type decking. The wheels look anything but round and have iron tyres, with the lever hand-brake acting on the outside. The cupboard under the bench seat probably contained tools, ropes and even the carman's lunch. The driver was his own mechanic, half a day every week being devoted to overhaul and adjustments. Most uniforms were of leather, complete with gaiters, and this was the only protection from the weather. The load looks very insecure and does not appear to be roped.

Below: A view of A-7645, this time loaded with fish boxes. One can imagine this primitive vehicle with low bonnet and oil lamps on its journey between Paddington and Billingsgate, a regular run, rattling over the cobbled streets up to an unofficial 20mph. For this traffic the lorry was fitted with special sides. The actual fleet number of this vehicle was thought to have been 37, but, as can be seen, the registration number was used.

Above: In July 1905, in association with the Teme Valley Agricultural Association, the steam wagon and trailer shown here was placed in service at Henwick, Worcester. It was supplied by the Yorkshire Patent Steam Wagon Company Ltd of Hunslet, Leeds, and its main function was to convey market produce etc between the railway and the local agriculturists' association depots.

Below: A works photograph of the Yorkshire Patent Wagon vehicle, this time without its trailer. Note the speed limit of 5mph.

Above: **A Plymouth-registered Milnes-Daimler 30hp goods lorry at Penzance** (date not known but almost certainly 1905). Judging by the interest shown by both the bowler-hatted and other staff, the vehicle had only just been delivered and was fairly new. The wheels still have iron tyres, and the distinctly railway-type screw brake was fitted in addition to a hand-brake.

Above: This superb photograph shows the first motor parcels van in service on the GWR. It was built by the Wolseley Tool & Motor Car Co Ltd of Birmingham, and is depicted here in one of the many squares near Paddington station in 1905. This vehicle had chain drive and the wheels were fitted with solid rubber tyres, single at the front, double at the back. The gold-leaf shaded lettering is an excellent example of the signwriter's art. The carman appears to be in an ordinary suit.

Below: During 1906 an electric wagon was purchased from the USA on the recommendation of the Chief Goods Manager after his visit to that country. This vehicle was almost certainly built by the Riker Electric Vehicle Company of Elizabethport, New Jersey, and was in use in the United States. This electric wagon had a 2-ton capacity and was used for collection and delivery of light goods in London. It was propelled by two enclosed electric motors with a current of 80 volts.

Above and below: After the American vehicle had been put through its paces for a couple of years, the GWR built its own version, as seen here. Fleet No 95, a new type of electric lorry for parcels and goods delivery work, is in service at Paddington on 8 June 1908. It was built at the Motor Car Department workshops at Slough and had many improvements on the USA type. It was driven by a 40-cell battery, giving it a capacity of about 30 miles on one charge. Note the calliper brakes working on the motor shaft, while the wheels have 4-inch-thick solid rubber tyres. The load was not to exceed 2 tons, and in the second photograph it comprises crates of tobacco from W. D. & H. O. Wills.

The Great Western Railway Motor-Car Department—II.

OFFICE METHODS.

BY W. BAILEY.

THE Department had, of course, to commence without the advantage of precedents based on experience of road motor working, and, therefore, railway practice was followed as far as circumstances permitted. Departures from usual railway office methods were, however, inevitable. Among the

The card system is largely utilised in the office, and found to be invaluable as a means of keeping records in a compressed and readily accessible form. This will be seen from the " Tyre Card," reproduced below. Tyres are usually purchased and paid for on a mileage basis, which necessitates a separate record being kept of the mileage run by each tyre (some 600 in all) and of the wheel changes made when a tyre fails or a wheel requires repair.

A careful check is kept on the use of " con-

Specimen Card Records used in Motor-Car Department.

new forms that have been devised, a special feature is made of the " Daily Report," which is despatched by each leading driver by the last available train (or, in the case of some of the more remote centres, by post) to enable it to reach the office at Slough early next morning. This form, a specimen of which is reproduced, gives at a glance the conditions prevailing at each depôt on the previous day.

sumable stores "—i.e., petrol, oil, grease, etc. These are ordered by the leading drivers weekly on a special form. A list showing the position, in the matter of economy of consumption, in order of merit of each depôt, and of each of the three divisions into which the services are divided, is issued each four weeks, and a commendable rivalry is thus fostered between the men in this important respect.

Above: Copy of a page which appeared in the *Great Western Railway Magazine* in September 1910 giving details of the administration backup required to run the Motor Car Department.

Above: Vehicle No 109, which entered service in 1910, was officially known as a motor parcel cart! The chassis was built by Sidney Straker & Squire Ltd of London, with the body manufactured at Swindon Works, where the photograph was taken on 23 November 1909, and entered service in 1910. Six of these vans were put to work in the Birkenhead area, fitted with two-cylinder vertical engines developing 14hp and designed to carry 15cwt; the speed was 15mph. The carman was afforded better weather protection with a front screen and canopy, and the wheels were fitted with Dunlop solid rubber tyres. Notice the double royal poster advertising the ferry service to Ireland from Fishguard, a passage of less than 3 hours.

Below: A nearside view of a similar vehicle, prior to being allocated a fleet number. The silencer runs across the vehicle instead of in-line.

Above: A letter and specification for a 5-ton chassis, sent to the GWR in 1911.

Below: Milnes-Daimler 30 hp 3½-ton goods lorry No 49, fitted with an experimental body for work in London, circa 1911.

Above and left: During 1919 the GWR put into service further types of electric vehicles for goods and cartage work. In order to obtain information on the actual working of electric propulsion, the company purchased four 5-ton vehicles for goods, built by the General Vehicle Co, Tyseley, Birmingham, and two 3$\frac{1}{2}$-tonners, four 2$\frac{1}{2}$-tonners and one 1$\frac{1}{2}$-tonner, all for parcels and built by Ransome, Sims & Jefferies Ltd of Ipswich. These two photographs show three of the 2$\frac{1}{2}$-ton 'Orwell' electric parcel vans, Nos E-11, E-12 and E-14, at Paddington. The driver's cab, which was fixed to the chassis, was a standard type for electric vehicles and was designed by the GWR Motor Car Department; it afforded good protection for the driver without restricting his vision. The load-carrying bodies, built at Swindon, were easily removable. The paint date on all three is 24 March 1919, and the livery appears to be crimson lake with the garter coat of arms (with crest on either side) on the cabside and shaded GWR lettering on the front; the tilt is black with white letters. On the frontal view vehicle E-14 has rear mudguards whereas the others have not. As can be seen, two traction motors drove the front wheels and, naturally, the vans had electric lights. The speed was 9-14mph.

Left: Another view of 2$\frac{1}{2}$-ton electric parcels van No E-11. Built by Ransome (Works No 1058), it was photographed in 1919. The batteries are Exide 'Ironclads'.

Right: An offside view of 2¹/₂-ton 'Orwell' electric parcels van No E-14, Ransome's Works No 1068, photographed at Swindon on 3 July 1919. No electric lamps are fitted, and the load is not to exceed 2t 10cwt.

Right: Electric parcels van No E-13 having the electrolyte in the battery checked prior to being charged. Note how easy it was to slide the batteries out for examination. The photograph was taken at Westbourne Park circa 1920.

Right: One of the 5-ton electric vehicles built by the General Vehicle Co, Tyseley, Birmingham. Numbered E-5 in the GWR fleet and fitted with a Swindon flat body, it was photographed in 1919. The difference between this vehicle and those built by Ransome is the fact that this one is propelled by a chain-drive to the rear axle.

Above: A 20hp Straker Squire parcels van, Fleet No 308, somewhere in the London area around 1915, complete with lady driver. It is well known that the railway recruited women for duties during World War 1, and many were employed in the Road Vehicle Department.

Below: Straker Squire 1-ton 14hp parcels van No 142 photographed in Cardiff, running on coal gas. Quite a number of road vehicles, both goods and passenger, were so converted during World War 1. It was found that the forward movement of the vehicle tended to drive the gas to the rear of the bag, so it was drawn off at the back, necessitating the ugly pipe along the side.

Above: A fine example of the Road Motor Constructor's art, a 1-ton parcel van, No 527, based on a 30cwt chassis supplied by H. G. Burford & Co Ltd of North Kensington, London. The 10cwt body was built at Swindon Works, and the photograph was taken at Westbourne Park on 17 October 1922, by which time 14 of this type had been built. The body portion was constructed of timber, the tilt being made of light matchboarding covered in canvas. Wings over the solid-rubber-tyred wheels had a combined running board at the front. In this example the tilt is painted cream, with the main body chocolate brown; the lettering also appears to be brown.

Below: A 1923 dimensional drawing of a Burford 30cwt chassis for the use of the body builder.

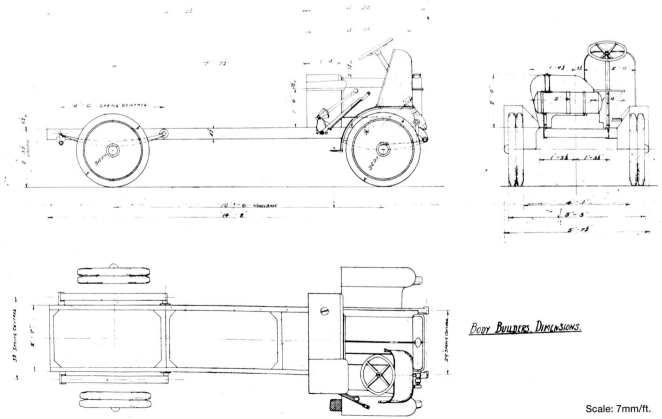

BODY BUILDERS. DIMENSIONS.

Scale: 7mm/ft.

Above: **How to load a lorry to the utmost – low bridges beware! I could not resist this very dilapidated photograph – did the photographer deliberately place the lorry and load to coincide exactly with the gable of the building behind? The flat lorry is a 3½-ton AEC thought to be in the Hereford area in the early 1920s. Why did staff so often stand in front of the fleet number?**

Below: **The Motor Vehicle Garage and Workshop at Alfred Road, Westbourne Park, London, was authorised in 1920 and partly completed in the same year. This photograph, taken on 30 September 1920, shows one of the three service bays. It appears that the vehicles, including Straker Squires and AECs, are undergoing cleaning, which was apparently all done with buckets and brushes, no hoses being used. The number of vehicles at the depot at that time was as follows:**

Capacity	Type	Goods	Parcels
1 ton	Petrol	–	16
1½ tons	Petrol	–	11
3½ tons	Petrol	59	11
5 tons	Petrol	2	–
2½ tons	Electric	–	4
3½ tons	Electric	–	2

Top and above: AEC 3½-ton lorry No 644 photographed in the early 1920s. These were ex-Army vehicles, of which 130 were purchased second-hand by the GWR after World War 1. The flat body and cab were manufactured by the GWR, and although one couldn't possibly call them handsome, they were very reliable vehicles and proved, when fitted with special sides, the most suitable for the cartage of sugar beet. This chassis was one of those used with charabanc bodies in summer, and reverting to goods work in the winter. It can be seen that the chassis has been recently repainted but the body has not.

Below: Another view of an AEC 3½-ton lorry, No 801, photographed on 28 September 1921; the Swindon paint date is 18 September 1921. In this case the body has sides and is fitted with a canvas tilt. These vehicles had 45bhp engines and the gearboxes had four forward speeds and reverse. A contemporary advertisement by the Associated Equipment Co Ltd stated that these vehicles when new cost £1,075, and that 10,000 had been supplied to the War Department. The Walthamstow factory produced one chassis every half-hour.

Above: A line-up of seven AEC 3¹/₂-ton lorries shortly after delivery, probably in 1921.

Below: A detailed drawing of an AEC chassis.

Scale: 7mm/ft.

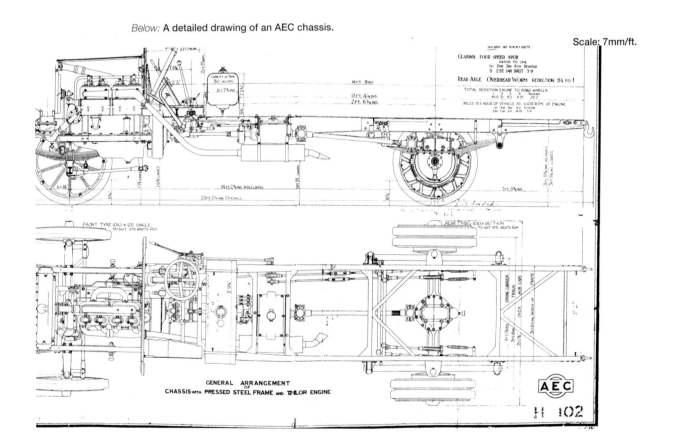

Above: A 3-ton Thornycroft parcel van, No C-1, photographed on 28 September 1921. The body and tilt are very similar to that fitted to the Straker Squire vehicle described earlier. The webs on the back wheels are of interest, as is the poster dated July 1921: 'Luggage in Advance 3/-' (15p). In those days your luggage arrived at its destination before your holiday ended!

Centre right and right: An example of a 30cwt D-type Burford forward-control flat lorry, No 574, photographed at Swindon Works after completion of the body and cab on 22 November 1923. The engine cover and bonnet are lined out and the paint date is 15 November 1923.

Above and below: Two views of Thornycroft A1 30cwt flat platform lorry No 947, with a body built at Swindon in 1926. The hoops could be fitted into the brackets along the length of the body, and the tarpaulin on the cab roof was thrown over to complete the outfit when loaded. A fire extinguisher is fitted in the cab. Photographed on 25 March 1926.

Left: A rather nice April 1926 view of a battered 30cwt Burford lorry, Fleet No 523, with a high-sided platform body. It had been outshopped from Swindon on 13 February 1925 – the cartage fleet certainly worked its vehicles hard.

Above: **An immaculate Model T Ford, No 331, fitted with a flat body supplied with the chassis. Note that the rear tyres are solid and the front are Goodrich pneumatic. The vehicle is also fitted with electric headlamps and the livery is all-over brown with cream lettering using a serif typeface. The photograph was taken on 17 March 1922.**

Right and below: **This is one of the nicest-looking motor vans produced in the 1920s, with a 30cwt A1 chassis supplied by John I. Thornycroft & Co Ltd of Basingstoke and a body built at Swindon Works. This photograph of 30cwt parcel van No 950 was taken on 25 March 1926, the paint date being 6 March 1926. The wheels are still fitted with solid rubber tyres, but the front wings are now moulded instead of the plain flat type. Oil lamps are supplied for side lighting only, and the speed is 12mph – quite fast enough after dark! The driver is provided with cushions – quite a luxury after the hard seats of previous types.**

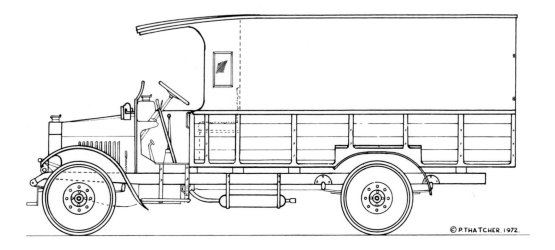

Scale 7mm/1ft

© P.THATCHER.1972.

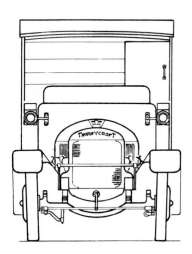

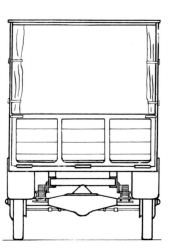

FEET

Above: Scale drawing of the Thornycroft A1 Motor Parcels Van.

Above: The difference in time between this photograph and those on the previous pages is 18 months. This 30cwt Thornycroft parcels van, No 981, on an A1 chassis, was photographed at Swindon Works on 5 October 1927. It is almost identical to No 950, but the major improvement is the provision of Dunlop pneumatic tyres, and in consequence the driver has lost his soft cushions. Another development is the fitting of electric head and sidelamps; brackets are still provided for oil lamps, however, as the Great Western always believed in wearing both belt and braces! The line of the roof is slightly more curved over the cab area, giving more protection from the weather.

Centre right and right: A superlative Great Western/Thornycroft combination, photographed in the late 1920s. This 30cwt van with an A1 chassis was probably one of the large number ordered for the Railhead schemes started in 1928. The main differences are the doors fitted to the side of the cab, the installation of a windscreen and the electrification of the side and rear oil lamps; the speed was uprated to 20mph. The body is No G1500, but the chassis bears the number 2000, which was to be the new fleet number later. It was the practice at that time to paint the tyre walls white and on occasions brick red!

This page: **A 4-ton 45hp PB forward-control chassis complete with cab, built by Thornycroft and shown outside that company's works at Basingstoke in 1927. Fifty of these chassis were delivered in that year, and they followed up-to-date practice in being fitted with an engine of 45hp that had a detachable head, automatic ignition and thermostatic control of the cooling water. The driver was placed alongside the engine, thus reducing the overall length and the amount of space the vehicle occupied, but the lorry still had the maximum floor space, which was an important factor in the restricted areas of goods yards and trading places. The photographs overleaf show the lorry completed and in service.**

Right and centre right: **These two pictures show Fleet No 1301, one of the batch referred to on the previous page, in service after the platform body had been fitted at Swindon. Taken in 1927, the photographs show clearly the stacking arrangement for the hoops. The vehicle behind, No 422, is an AEC.**

Below: **This photograph, according to the official records, was taken at Slough Works on 9 November 1927. No 1016 looks like a Model A Ford, but it is understood that the Model A Ford arrived on the scene in 1928! It is fitted with a very sombre body, not reminiscent of Swindon at all – did the Great Western ever run an undertaking business? The wheels are fitted with pneumatic tyres, there are electric headlamps and the usual oil sidelamps. The livery could be all-over brown or even black, while the letters are cut from brass and screwed into place. The fleet number appears to be vitreous enamel and riveted on.**

Above: Fleet No 1022 has the same chassis and cab as the vehicle in the previous picture, but this time is fitted with a Swindon-built high-sided body, without the hoop sticks and tarpaulin. The livery is again all brown or black, and the lettering is also as before, plus a signwritten 'GWR' on the body side and in front of the windscreen. It was also photographed at Slough on 9 November 1927.

Left: No 1307, a 4-ton 45hp Thornycroft road motor lorry, is fitted with a high-sided body built at Swindon Works, and hoops are provided to support the tarpaulin when required. Fitted with solid-rubber-tyred wheels and electric headlamps, plus brackets for oil lamps, the major difference is the forward-control system for steering, enabling the driver to be positioned further forward beside the engine, thereby giving more room for loads on the same chassis.

Left: No 578 is a 30cwt Burford forward-control chassis fitted with Swindon parcels van body, photographed on 25 March 1926. The protective tarpaulin makes the driver look as though he has retired for the night! The wheel design is interesting as it appears to be a compromise between the old horse-drawn wagon type and the new-style motor vehicle variety

Above: A view taken in a corner of the inwards shed at Birmingham (Hockley) Goods Yard during April 1927. Forward-control 30cwt Burford flat-bodied lorry No 546 is shown in the foreground, while beyond are a 4-ton Thornycroft, a 3½-ton AEC and another 4-ton Thornycroft.

Demountable Bodies

In the late 1920s experiments were carried out by the GWR into demountable bodies and movable tilts on lorries, all to expedite loading and to create a quicker turnround of vehicles. The idea was thought up by the Great Western Railway in 1925 and inaugurated in 1928 on a working basis.

The sum of £5,000 was originally voted by the GWR Board for the experiment. A 90-foot demountable stand was constructed at South Lambeth Goods Depot, adjacent and parallel to the loading platform, to deal with eight demountable bodies, with an hydraulic lifting rig midway in the centre. In operation the vehicle backed into the lifting bay guided by rails, and two roller-fitted lifting bars were 'shot' between the chassis and the body, which was then lifted hydraulically and pushed by hand on to the roller-fitted stand to either left or right, and a loaded or empty body pushed into place and lowered. The lifting bars were then retracted and the vehicle driven out for its next journey. This operation took just 2 minutes.

As a result of this experiment 200 new vehicles were purchased, and the demountable bodies for them were built at the GWR Carriage & Wagon Works at Swindon.

Above and below: Fleet No 828 is a 30cwt Burford forward-control chassis with a 'Coventry' demountable body. Note that the wheels on the lorry are of a solid type rather than spoked. This picture shows the original system being demonstrated at South Lambeth Goods Depot on 10 November 1927.

Above: Fleet No 1706, a 4-ton Thornycroft forward-control chassis fitted with a demountable body, is using the later more permanent system at South Lambeth Goods Depot on 4 April 1929. When the 'mechanical horse' and trailer vehicles arrived in the 1930s they replaced these experiments.

Below: A 30cwt Thornycroft forward-control vehicle, Fleet No 1815, using the demountable system circa 1929.

Above and below: **No 1334, a 4-ton Thornycroft forward-control chassis fitted with a sliding tilt supplied by the Portsmouth Motor Company, is seen on 26 May 1927 at a depot thought to be Park Royal. The tilt was constructed to enable the driver or loading staff to slide it forward so as to leave three-quarters of the loading space open. When closed, complete weather protection was provided. Quite a number of vehicles were fitted in this way.**

Road Motor Department Repair Shops, Slough

These shops were originally set up in 1905, but owing to the increase in the fleet of motors it became apparent that the existing accommodation was not sufficient. In 1926 a new brick structure was erected close to the old premises, 228 feet long by 81 feet wide with additional smaller bays to accommodate the smithy and engine testing apparatus. All the work was done under one roof, from the initial stripping down and cleaning to the final painting and varnishing. For the latter operations an area was totally screened off to exclude dust. A number of additional machines were installed, the most important being a cylinder grinder, which was capable of reboring the cylinders of any vehicle used by the GWR. Another new machine was a vulcanising plant for repairing damaged pneumatic tyres. The most interesting innovation was the lifting gantries, made at Slough, which were built to bridge any vehicle and were used for slinging heavy components, such as engines, in and out of the chassis. These gantries could be moved either in a longitudinal or lateral direction and even slewed round.

Above and below: The Road Motor Department Repair Shops at Slough as they looked in April 1927. The first photograph shows the exterior of the shops and the new office block, with the running shed in the distance, while the second gives an idea of the repair shop interior. The private car was for the use of the Road Motor Superintendent.

Chapter 4:
The Country Lorry Services

The Great Western Railway started the first of its country lorry services about the year 1908, between New Quay and Llandyssul and between Haverfordwest and St David's. The reason for this move was to provide better accommodation for parcels and goods traffic, which was proving too heavy for the roofs of the omnibuses. The two previously mentioned services, together with those operating at St Austell, Helston, Penzance, St Clears and Montgomery, were definitely scheduled to run on specific days and times. This was unlike the general pattern, where lorry journeys were varied from day to day according to requirements.

INDEX OF STATIONS AT WHICH LORRY SERVICES ARE IN OPERATION.

	SCALE OF CHARGES			SCALE OF CHARGES	
	2 or 4 ton lots see page	1 ton and less see page		2 or 4 ton lots see page	1 ton and less see page
Abergavenny	3	6	Llandyssul	3	8
Aberystwyth	3	6	Llansantffraid	3	6
*Albrighton	3	6	Ludlow	4	6
*Andoversford	3	6	Machynlleth	3	6
Ashburton	3	6	Maidenhead	3	6
Athelney	3	6	Market Drayton	4	6
Axbridge	3	6	Marlborough	3	6
Aylesbury	4	6	Martock	3	6
Badminton	4	6	Mathry Road	3	8
Bala	3	6	Melksham	3	6
Banbury	4	6	Midsomer Norton	5	5 & 6
Barnstaple	4	8	Minehead	3	6
*Baschurch	3	6	Monmouth	3	6
Bedwyn	3	6	Montgomery	3	8
*Berrington S.V.	3	6	Moreton-in-Marsh	3	6
Bewdley	3	6	*Much Wenlock	3	6
Bishop's Lydeard	3	6	Newbury	3	6
Blaenau Festiniog	4	6	Newcastle Emlyn	3	8
*Bourton-on-Water	3	6	*Newent	3	6
Bridgnorth	3	6	Newton Abbot	3	6
Bridgwater	5	5 & 6	Newtown	3	6
Bridport	4	6	Norton Fitzwarren	3	6
Bromyard	3	6	Oswestry	3	6
Buckfastleigh	3	6	*Penzance	3	7
Calne	3	6	Pershore	3	6
Castle Cary	3	6	Portmadoc	3	6
Charlbury	3	6	Presthope	3	6
Cheddar	3	6	Puxton & Worle	3	6
Cheltenham	4	6	Pwllheli	3	6
Chepstow	3	6	Radstock	5	5 & 6
Chippenham	4	6	Redruth	3	6
*Chirk	3	6	*Ross	3	6
Church Stretton	4	6	Rossett	3	6
*Cirencester	3	6	Ruabon	3	6
Clevedon	3	6	St. Austell	3	7
Codsall	3	6	St. Clears	3	6
Colwall	3	6	Salisbury	4	6
Corwen	4	6	Saltash	3	6
Craven Arms	4	6	Shifnal	3	6
*Crudgington	3	6	Shipston-on-Stour	3	6
Cullompton	3	6	Shipton	3	6
Dartmouth	3	6	Shrivenham	3	6
Devizes	3	6	Slough	3	6
Didcot	3	6	Somerton (Som.)	3	6
*Dolgelley	3	6	Southam Road	3	6
Dorchester	4	6	South Molton	3	6
Dulverton	3	6	Stourbridge	3	6
Dymock	3	6	Stourport	3	6
Ellesmere	3	6	Stratford-on-Avon	4	6
Evesham	4	6	Stroud	9	9
Fairford	3	6	Swindon	3	6
Faringdon	3	6	Talgarth	3	6
Four Crosses	3	6	Taunton	3	6
Frome	4	6	*Tenbury Wells	4	6
*Gloucester	4	6	Tetbury	3	6
Hallatrow	3	6	*Thame	3	6
Hartlebury	3	6	Theale	3	6
Haverfordwest	3	8	‡Thorverton	3	6
Helston	3	7	Tiddington	3	6
Henley-in-Arden	3	6	Tiverton	3	6
Henley-on-Thames	3	6	Tiverton Junction	3	6
Henllan	3	8	Totnes	3	6
Henwick	4	6	Trawsfynydd	3	6
*Hereford	4	6	Trowbridge	3	6
Highbridge	5	5 & 6	Truro	3	6
Hungerford	3	6	Wantage Road	3	6
Ilminster	3	6	Warminster	3	6
Ivybridge	3	6	Warwick	4	6
Keynsham	3	6	Wellington, Som.	3	6
Kidderminster	3	6	Welshpool	3	6
Kilgetty	3	6	Westbury, Wilts.	4	6
Kingsbridge	3	7	Weston super Mare	3	6
Kingswear	3	6	Winchester (See King's Worthy)		
King's Worthy	3	6			
*Kington	3	6	Witney	3	6
*Langport West	3	6	Wiveliscombe	3	6
Lavington	3	6	Wolverh'ton to Bridgnorth	3	6
Leamington	4	6	Woodborough	3	6
Lechlade	3	6	Wootton Bassett	3	6
Ledbury	3	6	Worcester	4	6
*Leominster	4	6	Yatton	3	6
Liskeard	3	6	Yeovil	4	6

All above Stations are connected by Telephone with the exception of Kilgetty.
‡Also operates service from Hele, Silverton, Cadeleigh and Stoke Canon.
*Stations marked thus are provided with Lorries specially equipped for dealing with livestock.

SCALE OF CHARGES FOR 2 AND 4 TON LOADS
applicable to the following Stations.

Abergavenny	Dolgelley	Machynlleth	Shifnal
Aberystwyth	Dulverton	Maidenhead	Shipston-on-Stour
Albrighton	Dymock	Marlborough	Shipton
Andoversford	Ellesmere	Martock	Shrivenham
Ashburton	Fairford	Mathry Road	Slough
Athelney	Faringdon	Melksham	Somerton (Som.)
Axbridge	Four Crosses	Minehead	Southam Road
Bala	Hallatrow	Monmouth	Stourbridge
Baschurch	Hartlebury	Montgomery	Stourport
Bedwyn	Haverfordwest	Moreton-in-Marsh	South Molton
Berrington S.V.	Helston	Much Wenlock	Swindon
Bewdley	Henley-in-Arden	Newbury	Talgarth
Bishop's Lydeard	Henley-on-Thames	Newcastle Emlyn	Taunton
Bourton-on-Water	Henllan	Newent	Tetbury
Bridgnorth	Hungerford	Newton Abbot	Thame
Bromyard	Ilminster	Newtown	Thorverton
Buckfastleigh	Ivybridge	Norton	Tiddington
Calne	Keynsham	Fitzwarren	Tiverton
Castle Cary	Kidderminster	Oswestry	Tiverton Junction
Charlbury	Kilgetty	Penzance	Totnes
Cheddar	*Kingsbridge	Pershore	Trawsfynydd
Chepstow	Kingswear	Portmadoc	Truro
Chirk	King's Worthy	Presthope	Wantage Road
Cirencester	Kington	Puxton & Worle	Wellington, Som.
Clevedon	Langport West	Pwllheli	Weston-super-Mare
Codsall	Lavington	Redruth	Witney {Mare
Colwall	Lechlade	Ross	Wiveliscombe
Crudgington	Ledbury	Rossett	Wolverhampton
Cullompton	Liskeard	Ruabon	to Bridgnorth
†Dartmouth	Llandyssul	St. Austell	Woodborough
Devizes	Llansantffraid	St. Clears	Wootton Bassett
Didcot	Ludlow	Saltash	Yatton

DISTANCE.		2-ton loads per ton.	4-ton loads per ton.
		s. d.	s. d.
Up to 1 mile		2 6	2 6
1 mile to 2 miles		3 0	2 6
2 miles to 3 miles		3 6	2 6
3 ,, 4 ,,		4 6	3 6
4 ,, 5 ,,		5 6	3 6
5 ,, 6 ,,		6 3	4 6
6 ,, 7 ,,		7 0	5 0
7 ,, 8 ,,		7 9	5 6
8 ,, 9 ,,		8 6	6 0
9 ,, 10 ,,		9 6	6 6
10 ,, 11 ,,		10 0	7 0
11 ,, 12 ,,		10 6	7 6
12 ,, 15 ,,		12 6	9 0
15 ,, 20 ,,		15 6	11 6

* The scale for distances over 15 miles does not apply to the Kingsbridge service.
† Traffic in classes 1-10 (except such traffics as loose bricks, tiles, stone, slates, etc., for which separate quotations will be given) will be delivered to Dartmouth and district by G.W. Country Lorry Service at the charges above increased by 2/4 per ton (minimum charge as for 2 tons) representing the Ferry charge between Kingswear and Dartmouth. For smaller consignments and all other traffic charged at Kingswear Station rates, the additional charge for ferrying to Dartmouth will be 4/- per ton, subject to the Cartage Scale on page 6 for lots of less than 2 tons.

Above and left: Extracts from a GWR Country Road Services booklet of 1936.

Unfortunately, failures occurred with the very early country lorry experiments, and real progress was not made until 1925. From then on, the service went from strength to strength, due, possibly, to the fact that roads were becoming unsuitable for horses, and also that motor transport was proving more exacting, and the rural community readily responded to the idea. The following statistics give some information on the number of services established during 1925-30:

To December 1925	8
To June 1926	12
To December 1926	19
To June 1927	29
To December 1927	45
To March 1928	57
To December 1930	120

Originally the services were inaugurated by the railway making an intensive canvass of farmers and others within a 10-mile radius of a station. However, as the country lorry service became better known, demand from a sufficient number of local residents served to justify a new service area.

The most suitable lorry for the work had a capacity of between 3½ and 4 tons, and the AECs, Thornycrofts and Associated Daimlers were known to have been utilised on these services, as the following photographs will show.

Another advantage of the country lorry service was the improvement effected in the clearance of rail wagons. Delays to wagons and resultant demurrage demands annoyed farmers and railways alike, and happened when private hauliers operated the scheme. Now the traffic was automatically delivered by the railway motor lorry shortly after the arrival of the wagon in the station siding.

One important factor in the success of the service was the appointment of a driver not only competent to deal efficiently with the railway company's clients, but also capable of carrying out the repair of minor mechanical defects in the case of breakdown. The lorries were expected to earn a small profit, although the basic idea was to feed the railway and assist in the development of country districts.

Another development was the cartage of milk traffic, which differed from the rest in requiring a carefully arranged timetable to ensure that milk, from a number of scattered farms, reached the railway station in time for a passenger train service. It was particularly necessary to ascertain that access to farms could be gained from the road; if not, arrangements were made to collect the milk from stages placed at the side of the road. This is still done today by the commercial successors to the Milk Marketing Board. It is interesting to note that one railway lorry carrying milk could displace four or more farmers' motor or horse vehicles, and this went some way to reducing wear and tear on country roads. The photographs of the Badminton service illustrate this point.

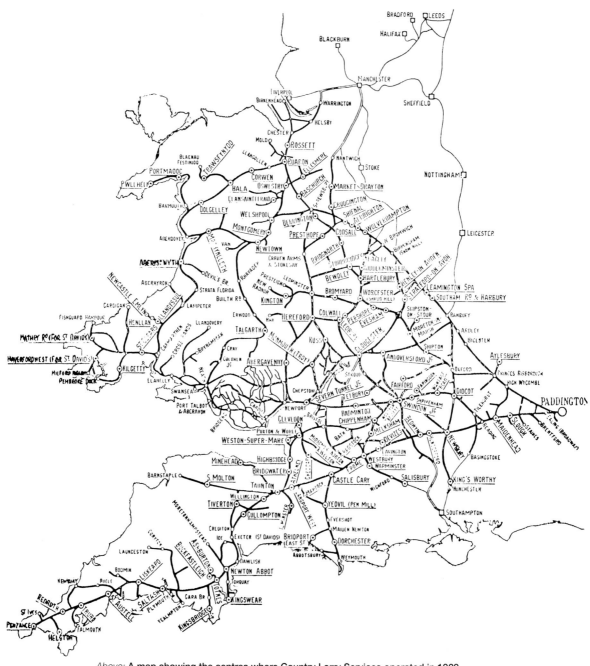

Above: **A map showing the centres where Country Lorry Services operated in 1929.**

64

Right: A double royal poster issued in July 1939 advertising the Country Lorry Services; it was produced using the pictures seen on pages 70-71. At this time the 'Big Four' railways had joined forces to promote their services.

Below: The vitreous enamel plates that were fitted to the lorries used on the Country Lorry Services vehicles; the upper one is original, while the small 'Station Master' plate is a replica. This example is on display in the Great Western Trust's Museum at Didcot.

Bottom: AEC 3½-ton lorry No 755 photographed at Badminton in February 1928 – note the enamel sign just described. In this instance the lorry was based at Badminton and is shown loaded with milk churns. In a report of January 1928 it was stated that at Badminton more than 700 gallons of milk were being brought in daily from farms within a radius of 5 miles, at a rate of ½d per imperial gallon. Note the acetylene headlamps, which were normally fitted to lorries working in country districts, and that the milk churns are of an early type.

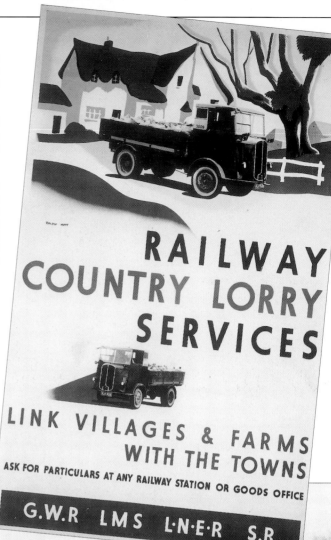

Above: No 1340, a 4-ton Thornycroft PB forward-control lorry, was also photographed at Badminton operating the Country Lorry Service, but in February 1928 and carrying the more modern type of milk churn. Acetylene headlamps are fitted, even though at this time Thornycroft was supplying the PB chassis with electric headlamps.

Centre right and right: AEC 3½-ton lorry No 685 engaged in delivering and unloading seed potatoes at a farm in the Albrighton area in September 1928 under the auspices of the Country Lorry Service. Note the different type of cab from that fitted to No 755 seen previously.

This page: Fleet No 1384, a 4-ton Thornycroft PB forward-control chassis fitted with a platform body, has slatted sides that were held by the brackets on the side of the body. These brackets were also used for holding the hoops, when supplied with tarpaulins. The rudimentary hand-operated jib was used to facilitate loading, in this instance milk churns. This lorry was based at Bewdley, and the photographs were taken there on 13 June 1929.

This page: **These two pictures show an AEC 3¹/₂-ton lorry, Fleet No 219, with flat body No G.916. The slatted sides are again held in the brackets provided; with the centre flap folded down it can be seen that the milk churns have been loaded in the normal way, but one wonders if the driver cornered fairly fast where some of the churns would end up! The lorry was based at Bedwyn and photographed there circa 1929. Note that a train has been signalled during the photographic session.**

This page: **Fleet No 1936, a 4/5-ton Associated Daimler chassis with a Swindon flat body, is seen operating the Country Lorry Service on 24 September 1929. The three photographs depict the vehicle offloading grain from an LMS open wagon, en route, then unloading at a farm in Woodhay.**

Above: Fleet No 2431 is a Thornycroft forward-control 2-ton chassis vehicle fitted with platform body G.1741, with detachable sides, and is seen on 16 January 1935 loading cooked flake maize at Lechlade. Here again the vehicle is operating the Country Lorry Service based on Lechlade.

Centre right and right: Fleet No 3009 is a Thornycroft 'Handy' 2-ton chassis with platform body G.2059 with drop-in high sides built at Swindon. The pictures were also taken on 16 January 1935 and show the vehicle on the Country Lorry Service loading grain at Lechlade and delivering it to a local farm. The Great Western Railway ordered 84 of these lorries, which had a 50hp side-valve petrol engine, a full floating rear axle and power-assisted brakes, very modern by any standard.

Above and below: **Fleet No 3009 is shown once again at Lechlade on the same date, 16 January 1935, this time fitted with a trailer.**

This page: Fleet No 1910, a 4/5-ton Associated Daimler chassis with a Swindon flat body (paint date 1 May 1929), is shown adapted for milk traffic and working on the Country Lorry Service in the Shrivenham area. The vehicle is first shown at Shrivenham station, then picking up milk at the roadside and finally loading churns at a nearby farm. The photographs were taken on 2 October 1929. The lorry is fitted with pneumatic tyres and a full windscreen, and as it probably did a lot of work in the dark (carrying milk), it is shown fitted with acetylene lamps as well as the oil variety. The petrol tank is under the driver's seat, hence the pipe in the cabside with the hefty cap secured by wing nuts.

Left: GWR fleet No 1938, a 4/5-ton Associated Daimler chassis fitted with a Swindon flat body and removable sides, is seen at the AEC works at Southall shortly after its paint date of 8 March 1929. It is interesting to note that the Daimler Motor Co Ltd joined forces with AEC from 1926 to 1929 to make Associated Daimler vehicles, then after 1929 Daimler concentrated on passenger vehicles. In this photograph it is noticeable that the offside door is held shut by a piece of wire attached to the mouth of the horn! There are no electric lights or windscreen, and the lorry is fitted with solid rubber tyres. The tarpaulin hoops are shown grouped together in the front bracket ready for use when required.

Left and below: Fleet No 1928 is another 4/5-ton Associated Daimler chassis fitted with Swindon flat body No G.1016, and was photographed on 15 March 1929, in the Birmingham area.

Above: Vehicle No 1992, a 4/5-ton Associated Daimler chassis, has no windscreen, but is fitted with a special 5-cubic-yard tipping body, which also had removable sides. The body is operated by a crank handle which fitted a shaft just in front of the rear wheels. Notice that there is a hole in the cabside where normally the petrol filler pipe and cap were found on other vehicles. Photographed on 6 October 1931, the livery appears to be all-over brown.

Right: Fleet No 1923 is a 4/5-ton Associated Daimler chassis with a van body. This vehicle, photographed in October 1930, has a full windscreen and pneumatic tyres.

Right: This 4/5-ton Associated Daimler chassis has a van body and is just out of the works – it certainly looks very smart compared to all the previous examples. Fleet No 1919 was photographed circa 1929 with Goodyear pneumatic tyres.

Above and below: Two official AEC photographs of a 4/5-ton Associated Daimler chassis as supplied to the GWR in 1929 before the bodies were fitted. The hinged cab arrangement is clearly shown.

Right and centre right: Another version of the 30cwt A1 chassis Thornycroft van adapted for contract hire, with a body built at Swindon. The Great Western Railway started contract hire in 1924 and the vehicles were for the sole use of the company concerned. As previously stated, the GWR entered into a contract with Macfarlane, Lang & Co in 1926, and this photograph of No 976 was taken at Redruth in January 1928. The vehicle bears standard GWR livery and lettering, and it appears that the firm's nameboard was interchangeable and could be fixed to any suitable vehicle. Other points of interest are the full windscreen and the roof-rack for biscuit tins. The cushion for the driver has been reinstated even though the van is fitted with pneumatic tyres. The vehicle has electric headlamps and sidelamps, as well as oil for standby, and its speed is 12mph.

Below: No 1347, a 4-ton Thornycroft van with solid tyres, electric headlamps and a full windscreen, is on contract hire to The India & China Tea Co, and bears that company's livery. The body was built at Swindon and photographed on 10 November 1927.

This page: **Contract hire par excellence:** No 979, a 30cwt Thornycroft chassis, has a Swindon body painted in Macfarlane, Lang & Co's own livery, thought to be green. Photographed at Bristol on 12 December 1928, it is fitted with footsteps and a handrail to enable the driver to reach the roof-rack – quite a job with a handful of 7lb empty biscuit tins! One way to see out of the cab during wet weather was to open the lower section – no windscreen wipers were fitted. The petrol filler cap can be seen next to the windscreen; the petrol tank was below the dashboard.

Above and below: **A further example of the expanding contract hire business is provided by No A 2518 in Macfarlane, Lang & Co's livery. Photographed at Exeter on 3 April 1936, the vehicle is a 2-ton Morris Commercial.**

Above: This 2-ton Dennis van, Fleet No 2339, is also on contract hire to Macfarlane, Lang and was photographed at Swindon on 24 July 1931.

Below: A dimensional drawing of the Dennis 2-ton chassis, dated 1930.

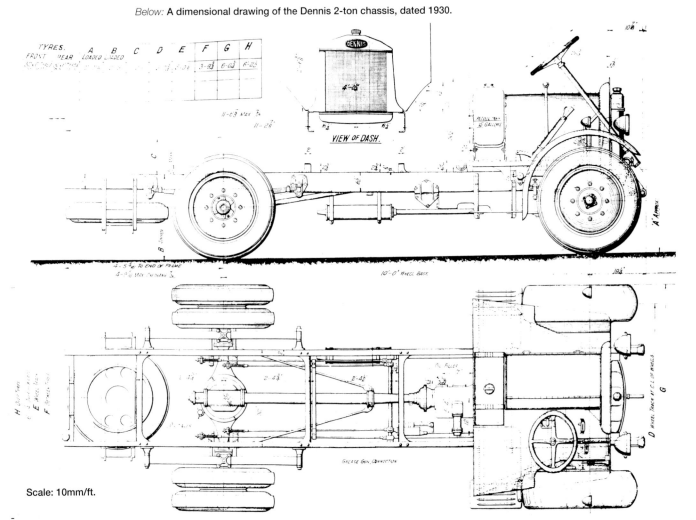

Scale: 10mm/ft.

Right and centre right: **Fleet No 2517** is a 2-ton Morris Commercial van, and is seen here at Exeter on 3 April 1936 on contract hire to Messrs Cadbury; it is painted in that firm's own livery.

Below: **Fleet No A 2233** is a 2-ton Morris Commercial forward-control van, also on contract to Messrs Cadbury and photographed at Swindon on 29 July 1927.

Left and below: **Fleet No 2330 is a 2-ton Dennis van, again in Cadbury's livery and photographed at Exeter in September 1930.**

Bottom: **Another Cadbury vehicle fresh out of the shops. This Morris Commercial was on contract hire, but bears the GWR Fleet No 2371. In this case the vehicle is branded 'Exeter Depot' and was photographed there in July 1931.**

Right and centre right: A 2-ton Morris Commercial van, numbered A 2520 in the GWR fleet, complete with roof-rack. It is shown here at Cardiff in 1936, on hire to Rowntree and painted in that company's own livery.

Below: A later 2-ton Morris Commercial van, Fleet No A2762, again on contract hire to Rowntree and photographed at Swindon on 6 April 1939.

Above: A 2-ton Dennis van of an unknown fleet number on contract hire to Kemps biscuits, another of the various companies that entered into contract hire with the GWR. It was photographed at Swindon on 23 December 1931; note the electrified oil sidelamps and very elaborate 3d lettering.

Centre left and left: A Morris Commercial forward-control chassis fitted with a van body for Kemps. Fleet No A2754, photographed on 30 May 1938, has a superb finish, as can be seen by the reflections on the sides.

Right: A Morris Commercial van on contract hire to Hughes & Co, another biscuit firm, photographed on 8 October 1931.

Below: Fleet No 1382 is a 4-ton Thornycroft PB forward-control lorry with a Swindon-built platform body and bearing a paint date of 3 May 1928. Thornycroft at this time produced the PB chassis with a 45hp engine. but if more power was required a 50hp engine was supplied, and it became the KC chassis.

Bottom: Another 4-ton Thornycroft PB forward-control chassis, Fleet No 1361, fitted with a high-sided flat body and a solid removable tilt. The paint date in this instance is 22 March 1928.

THORNYCROFT

4 TON (8,960 lbs.)

Types "PB" and "KC"

FREIGHT CHASSIS

General View of Type "PB" Chassis.

JOHN I. THORNYCROFT & CO., LIMITED

THORNYCROFT HOUSE, SMITH SQUARE, WESTMINSTER, S.W.1

Telephone: VICTORIA 8000. *Telegrams:* "THORNYCROFT, PARL, LONDON."

Works: BASINGSTOKE.

Home Depots for Repairs and Supplies of Spare Parts:

BIRMINGHAM: 91, New Canal Street. **GLASGOW:** 61, Bishop Street, Anderston. **LEEDS:** St. Michael's Lane, Headingley. **LONDON:** Pulford Street, Pimlico, S.W.1. **MANCHESTER:** Gt. Bridgewater Street, Deansgate. **NEWCASTLE-ON-TYNE:** 14, Higham Place

LIVERPOOL OFFICE: 15, Sweeting Street.

Overseas Branches:

Bombay, Cairo, Calcutta, Hong Kong, Johannesburg, Melbourne, Montreal, Rio de Janeiro, Sao Paulo, Shanghai, Singapore, Sydney, Tokyo.

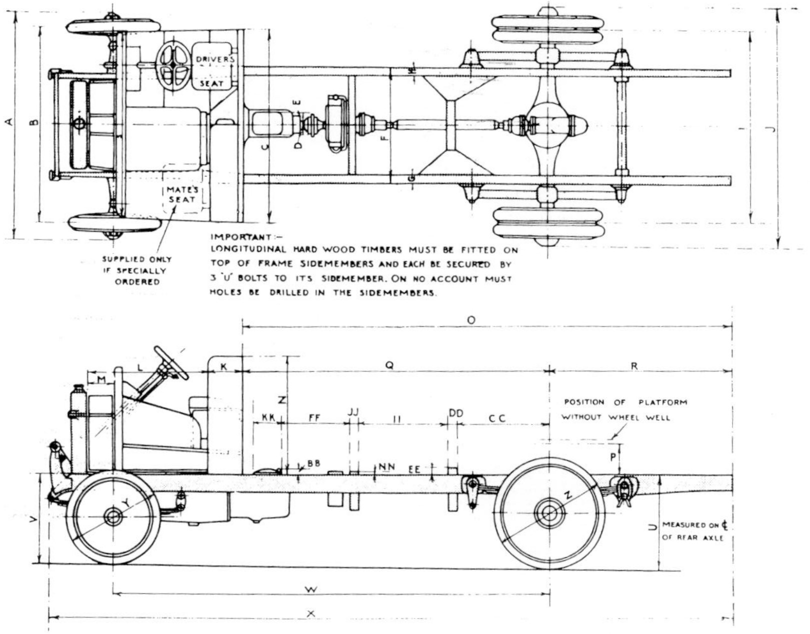

DRIVERS SEAT
MATES SEAT
SUPPLIED ONLY IF SPECIALLY ORDERED
IMPORTANT:— LONGITUDINAL HARD WOOD TIMBERS MUST BE FITTED ON TOP OF FRAME SIDEMEMBERS AND EACH BE SECURED BY 3 'U' BOLTS TO IT'S SIDEMEMBER. ON NO ACCOUNT MUST HOLES BE DRILLED IN THE SIDEMEMBERS.
POSITION OF PLATFORM WITHOUT WHEEL WELL
MEASURED ON ℄ OF REAR AXLE

Body Builders' Diagrams of THORNYCROFT

Types "PB" and "KC" Chassis

DIMENSIONS

On standard 34 ins. × 5 ins. and 40 ins. × 5 ins. solid tyres.

	ft.	ins.	metres.		ft.	ins.	metres.		ft.	ins.	metres.		ft.	ins.	metres.
A ...	6	10	2·083	J ...	7	2½	2·197	R ...	5	6	1·676	*Z ...	3	4¼	1·022
B ...	5	9	1·753	*J ...	7	5¼	2·267	S ...	5	8	1·727	BB ...		2	·051
*B ...	6	0¾	1·848	K ...		11¾	·298	U ...	2	9½	·851	CC ...	2	8½	·825
C ...	5	9¼	1·759	†L ...	3	8¼	1·124	*U ...	2	8½	·825	DD ...		3½	·089
D ...		4¼	·108	‡L ...	4	0¾	1·238	V ...	2	8½	·825	EE ...		2½	·063
E ...		4¼	·108	†M ...		10½	·267	*V ...	2	10½	·876	FF ...	2	6⅜	·772
F ...	3	6	1·067	‡M ...	1	3	·381	W ...	13	0	3·962	II ...	2	1⅜	·645
G ...		3	·076	N ...	3	7	1·092	X ...	20	5½	6·235	JJ ...		3	·076
H ...		3	·076	O ...	14	7½	4·458	Y ...	2	10	·864	KK ...		10¾	·273
I ...	5	9¼	1·759	P ...		10¾	·273	*Y ...	3	4¼	1·022	NN ...		1	·025
*I ...	6	0¾	1·848	Q ...	9	1½	2·781	Z ...	3	4	1·016				

* Varying Dimensions for alternative 38 ins. × 7 ins. Dunlop Pneumatic Tyres.

† Refers to type "PB" Chassis only. ‡ Refers to type "KC" Chassis only.

The above dimensions are subject to alteration, and should be confirmed by us before bodies are put in hand.

FOR PRICES, TERMS OF BUSINESS AND GUARANTEE, SEE PRICE LIST.

Above: Pages from a publicity hand-out concerning the PB and KC chassis issued by John I. Thornycroft & Co Ltd in January 1929.

Above and below: Two views of a 30cwt Thornycroft forward-control chassis fitted with a flat body, sides, and brackets in use with hoops and a partial tarpaulin. Numbered 1445 and bearing the Swindon paint date 22 June 1928, it was photographed at the Westbourne Park Road Motor Depot on 19 October 1928. The lever just in front of the rear wheels is presumably the device for anchoring the body to the chassis; most bodies were removable for maintenance, and to the left of the first picture a flat body is shown on trestles. Of interest in the second photograph is the heap of discarded solid rubber tyres.

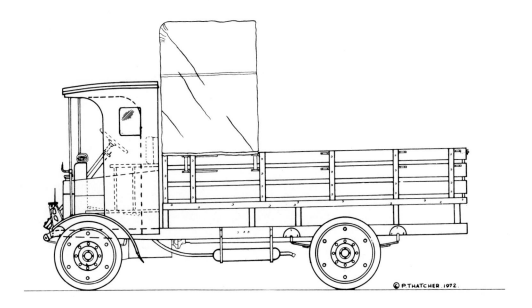

Scale 7mm/1ft

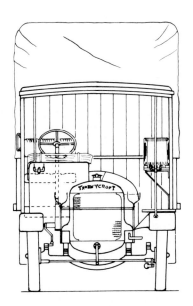

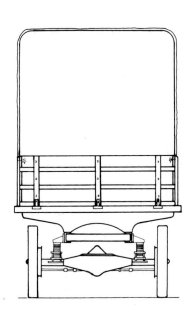

FEET

Above: **Scale drawing of the Thornycroft forward-control 30cwt motor lorry.**

Right and centre right: **This very nice lightweight motor parcels van, No 1122, is based on a chassis built by Morris Commercial Cars Ltd, Birmingham, with a body partly built at Swindon Works. The photograph was taken about 1928, and the vehicle is fitted with electric headlamps and sidelamps, pneumatic tyres and a full windscreen. It appears that the GWR thought that this vehicle's electric lamps were completely reliable as there is no provision for fixing oil lamps.**

Below: **This Morris Commercial 1-ton van, No 2507, with a production body, was photographed at Paddington in 1930. As can be seen, it was used mainly for baggage in connection with boat trains from Weymouth and Plymouth. The immaculate livery of brown and cream is very evident. With electric headlamps and sidelamps and pneumatic tyres, the vehicle looks very modern for the period. The petrol tank filler cap can be seen in front of the windscreen.**

Above and below: **This 4-ton Thornycroft PB chassis with a platform body is No 1323, and the photograph was taken in Chiseldon Goods Yard (M&SWJR) on 15 June 1928. The Stanton pipes were being conveyed in connection with the Swindon water pipeline. The Fordson tractor is similarly engaged with trailer No T 42, which has wheels from a scrapped road motor vehicle. The rail-mounted crane on a short length of track is of interest; note also North British Railway open wagon No 14937.**

Above: No 1857, a 30cwt Thornycroft forward-control chassis fitted with Swindon flat body (Swindon paint date 31 May 1929), is shown as running in October 1930. It is a very primitive-looking lorry considering the date, with no electric light and no windscreen. Instead of the usual Dunlop tyres this vehicle and that on page 86 are fitted with solid 'Henley Air Cushion' tyres. The GWR plate fitted to the bonnet was becoming standard at this time, and the signwriter evidently considered that there was not enough room for the full word 'Railway', as on some horse-drawn vehicles. The 'M' on the top of the cab is thought to denote that the vehicle belonged to the maintenance department.

Right: In 1929 the GWR took delivery of 100 30cwt forward-control A1 chassis from John I. Thornycroft & Co Ltd, and this photograph shows the vehicle at the firm's Basingstoke works, under test, on 1 November 1929, in temporary works livery and with a stencilled 'GWR' on the cab front.

Right: Fleet No 2007 was one of that batch, and is seen after Swindon Works had completed the van body and painted it ready for the road; in this instance the cab had been supplied by Thornycroft. It seems that at this time the lighter vehicles were fitted with pneumatic tyres. The photograph was taken at Swindon Works on 4 December 1929.

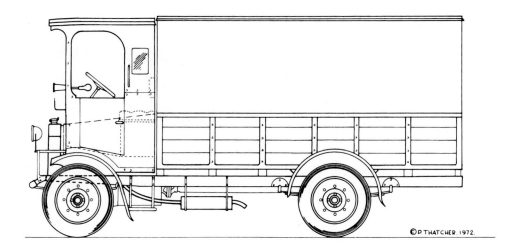

Scale 7mm/1ft

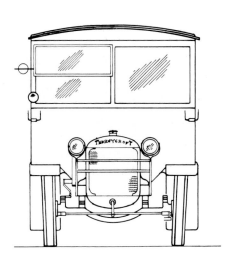

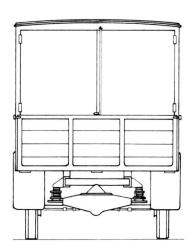

FEET

Above: **Scale drawing of a Thornycroft forward-control parcels van.**

Right: As well as the 30cwt chassis ordered from Thornycroft, 100 4-ton forward-control chassis were also delivered to the GWR in 1929, thereby making it one of the largest orders of this kind placed with the manufacturer. This picture shows one of the 4-ton chassis under test at Basingstoke on 1 November 1929, prior to delivery to the GWR. Solid tyres appear to be the order of the day for this weight of vehicle at the time.

Right: No 1716 is one of that batch of 4-ton chassis, seen here fitted with a GWR flat body with removable sides; bearing a Swindon paint date of 26 November 1929, it was photographed in October 1930. Brackets were fitted to the sides to carry the tarpaulin hoops, as shown.

Below: The Great Western station at Oswestry closed in July 1924, when all trains began to use the Cambrian Railways station. It is apparent from this photograph, taken on 7 November 1928, that the closed station was in use as a Road Vehicle Depot. Shown here are two AEC 3½-ton high-sided lorries, Nos 792 (left) and 260 (right); the latter had in fact been an omnibus and was fitted with a lorry body on 2 March 1927. The other vehicles under the canopy are No 936 (left), a Thornycroft single-deck omnibus, and another AEC lorry. Also seen in the photograph is a very nice selection of enamel signs and company wagons, including one from the Furness Railway.

Above: In 1929 it became apparent that equipment capable of hauling heavier loads in some districts of the GWR was required. Shown here is S-18, a 12-ton six-wheel steam wagon built by Foden Ltd, Elworth Works, Sandbach, Cheshire, and loaded with grain at Exeter in typical British weather on 6 December 1929. During 1929 four rigid-frame six-wheelers were supplied to the GWR; two were fitted with flat platform bodies 20 feet long, as here, and two with hydraulic three-way tipping bodies. They were designed for loads of 10-12 tons at 12mph or for gradients of 1 in 7 at corresponding speeds. The boiler worked at 220psi, the total heating surface was 90sq ft, and the compound engine had 4¼-inch and 7-inch diameter cylinders with a 7-inch stroke, but could be worked with live steam in both cylinders and independent exhaust when required.

Below: Fleet No S-20, seen in 1929, is one of the rigid-frame six-wheelers fitted with the three-way tipping bodies. The livery of these vehicles appears to be green and lined out.

Bottom: This AEC 3½-ton lorry, Fleet No 254, is about to unload sugar beet at Albrighton on 1 January 1929. Note the conveyor belt operated by the oil engine on the platform of the conveyor.

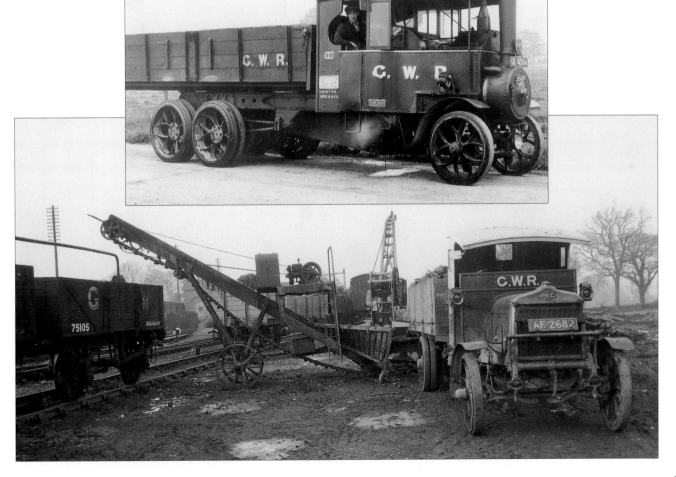

Above: This peculiar-looking Burford 30cwt forward-control flat lorry, No 875, has detachable sides and was photographed at Swindon Works on 22 February 1930. It was the result of a rebuild from an omnibus type similar to one shown on page 203 . Using the same chassis the bus coachwork was removed and a cartage body fitted in its place; many GWR motor omnibuses were converted in this way. The petrol tank is under the seat, and the word 'Railway' has again been abbreviated. This particular vehicle was finally withdrawn and scrapped in 1933.

Below: Another rebuild, this time an AEC 3½-ton chassis with flat body No 286 converted in 1927; fleet numbers were retained after conversion. The picture on page 199 shows how this vehicle looked as a charabanc, but it is seen here as a lorry in the goods yard at Torre on 27 May 1930 loading agricultural machinery for the Bath & West and Southern Counties Show at Torquay.

Above: As previously mentioned, the GWR was engaged in the cartage of gravel and sand from the jointly owned pits at Theale in Berkshire. One contract required the conveyance of 5,000 tons, so a large number of high-sided vehicles were required for this traffic and the majority were purchased from Thornycroft. This photograph shows a superb collection of road vehicles of this type assembled at Theale station in 1930. In the front row, from left to right, are a Foden steam wagon, a tractor and trailer, and a Thornycroft 10-ton six-wheeler. The remainder are mostly 4-ton Thornycrofts with solid rubber tyres, with one Associated Daimler on the extreme right.

Centre left: Theale & Great Western Sand & Ballast Company was the name given to the joint concern working the pits and conveying the material. Here is vehicle No 2247, a 7-ton Thornycroft chassis fitted with a 6½cu yd capacity steel hydraulic tipping body. The unladen weight shown on the cab is 6t 4cwt. The photograph, taken on 6 October 1931, depicts the vehicle tipping ballast on site during the construction of Tilehurst reservoir, Reading.

Left: No 1077, a Thornycroft JC 10-ton six-wheeler forward-control chassis fitted with a side-tipping steel hopper body, is seen at Theale station on 6 October 1931. Note the protective slats over the petrol tanks. Considering the date, this was a very modern-looking vehicle.

Right and centre right: **These two consecutively numbered Thornycroft JC forward-control six-wheelers, Nos 1078 and 1079, have Swindon-built 32cwt bodies with detachable sides. The chassis are 6t 1½cwt and the engine has six cylinders developing 45.9hp. When ordered in 1930 the cost was recorded as £1,400 each. The photographs were taken at Swindon, the first on 30 August 1933 and the second about 1935.**

Below: **Another six-wheeled forward-control Thornycroft JC chassis, photographed on 14 April 1930 and fitted with a full cab and a hinged high-sided body. The unladen weight is shown as 7t 3cwt 2qr, and it carries a roof board showing that it is working for the St Martin Preserving Co; further reference to this company's traffic will appear later in the book. Close scrutiny of the picture shows that the lorry is fitted with one windscreen wiper on the driver's side only. The livery appears to be all-over brown, and the photograph was taken on Front Hill, Paddington.**

Right: Fleet No 2249, body No G 1949, is a Thornycroft 5/6-ton forward-control JJ chassis fitted with a 6½cu yd tipper body. The livery appears to be either all-over brown or grey. The photograph, circa 1931, is thought to have been taken at Exeter.

Above: During 1931 the GWR extended its road freight services still further by taking delivery of 219 new motors and tractors ordered at a cost of £127,000. Of these 108 were built by Dennis Bros Ltd, Onslow Works, Guildford, being 20.36hp forward-control vehicles. This photograph shows the Dennis chassis being tested on a gradient of 1 in 6 on one of the hills overlooking Guildford on 31 May 1931.

Right: This Fordson Type B is fitted with a three-way tipper body. Five of these vehicles were purchased by the GWR to increase the fleet used in connection with the gravel pit traffic at Theale, where this example was photographed on 6 October 1931 with a fleet number not yet allocated.

Above: During 1932, at Lostwithiel, Cornwall, the Nestlé Company set up a milk concentration depot in the GWR station yard, a site that was convenient for the receipt of milk from farms by road and for despatch in bulk by rail in 3,000-gallon glass-lined tank wagons. Nestlé's contracted with about 600 farmers for daily supplies of milk up to a total of 7,000 gallons, and its collection each day, including Sundays, from such a scattered area presented a big problem, solved by the GWR taking over the whole contract from 1 October 1932. There were nine other small centres co-ordinated with the scheme, each having its own allocation of lorries; Lostwithiel, being the largest, had six vehicles. The road equipment used on the contract was almost entirely made up of 2-ton lorries, and this photograph shows, from left to right, a Thornycroft 2-tonner, a Morris Commercial 'Courier' high-sided 6-tonner, two more Thornycroft 2-tonners, and, on the extreme right, a special 6-ton Morris Commercial double-decked lorry for conveying 135 8-gallon churns used in the remote areas; the 2-ton vehicles carried about 50 8-gallon churns. Forty years later this sort of operation was carried out by the Milk Marketing Board using only its own road transport; British Rail carried only a very small percentage. Milk Mart is the present transport provider.

Centre right: A close-up of the 6-ton Morris Commercial double-decked lorry, Fleet No 2902, also photographed on 18 October 1932.

Rright: Another view of the Lostwithiel Milk Depot, in which one more vehicle is shown, Fleet No 1905, an Associated Daimler 4/5-ton lorry with a platform body. Photographed on 18 October 1932, it is still displaying the Country Lorry Service enamel plate.

Above and below: **Fleet No 2080 is a 30cwt forward-control Thornycroft chassis fitted with platform body No G.1590 and removable sides. This vehicle was one of the large batch delivered to the GWR in 1929; bearing a paint date of 3 March 1930, it was photographed in July 1931.**

Above and bottom: This 2-ton forward-control chassis, with a specially adapted radiator to combat overheating in hilly districts, was built by Guy Motors Ltd, Wolverhampton, provided with a Swindon van body and numbered 2350 in the GWR fleet. Fitted with electric headlamps, electrified oil lamps and horn, it was photographed in July 1931.

Right: This 2-ton Guy OND chassis represents another interesting conversion. Shown here as a motor lorry with detachable sides provided by Swindon, it was previously a saloon motor coach used by the GWR between Paddington and Victoria (see page 220), although its fleet number, 1651, was retained throughout. The photograph was taken on 23 August 1933 after its conversion with body No G.174.

Above and below: **These photographs show two 4-ton Thornycroft PB chassis fitted with platform bodies and detachable sides, the main difference between them being that one has solid tyres and the other pneumatic. They have full windscreens and electric lighting, and both Fleet Nos 1716 and 2106 were photographed in October 1930.**

Right: The transport of livestock in the 1930s was quite considerable and the railway companies had a good share in the operation. They were, however, very keen to increase it, and these two posters were issued by the GWR in November 1936.

LET US COLLECT AND DELIVER YOUR LIVE STOCK

PARTICULARS OF CHARGES BY ROAD OR RAIL FROM THE COMPANY'S REPRESENTATIVE AT THE MARKET OR YOUR LOCAL STATION

GWR

DO YOU KNOW WHAT "TACKING" SHEEP ARE? WE DO! — AND CAN CARRY THEM AND ANY OTHER ANIMALS

GWR

FOR INFORMATION REGARDING THE CONVEYANCE OF LIVESTOCK APPLY TO YOUR LOCAL GOODS AGENT OR STATION MASTER

Above and left: The first photograph is one of those taken circa 1935 to produce the posters; the vehicle is a 5/6-ton Thornycroft JJ forward-control chassis with a Tasker double-decker cattle body. In the second view the vehicle is seen at Swindon on 16 May 1931.

Above and below: **Fleet No 2477, a 2-ton Thornycroft forward-control chassis fitted with full-fronted cab, electric headlamps, electrified oil lamps, and pneumatic tyres, has Swindon utility-type livestock body G.1787, and the cab bears the Swindon paint date of 29 September 1932. Note the cast 'Great Western Railway' plates on the body side and the very small windscreen wiper. It was photographed at Thame on 17 November 1932.**

Right: A Bedford 2/3-ton chassis has been fitted with a combined horse box/cattle body built by Messrs Walters & Co of Rugby; the GWR body number is G.2032 and the Fleet No 1646. The vehicle is on contract hire to F. J. & H. T. Quartly of Thame, where the photograph was taken on 17 November 1932. Note the LNER touch of imitation teak livery on the bonnet and cab.

Right: This other Bedford vehicle, photographed at Thame on the same day, is also on contract hire to Quartly's; the body number is G.2031 and the Fleet No 1645. Note the slightly different cab.

Above: **Fleet No 2444**, a 30cwt Thornycroft chassis fitted with a cattle body, was photographed at Swindon on 23 September 1932 to demonstrate the open and closed positions. Notice the 'Great Western Railway' cast-iron plates on the sides instead of the usual signwritten variety.

Below and below left: **Fleet No 1550** is a 30hp forward-control Maudslay ML3 4/5-ton chassis with a double-decker cattle body. This vehicle was originally an omnibus, but was severely damaged by a large tree falling on it (see page 208) and was rebuilt as shown in December 1930 with bodywork by Messrs Tasker; the same fleet number was retained throughout. The vehicle had two decks for use in conveying small animals, but when required for cattle the top flooring could be removed. It is seen here at Slough.

Above: Fleet No B 4645 is a Thornycroft 'Sturdy' chassis fitted with a cattle body, and was photographed at Swindon on 28 November 1943. The livery appears to be all-over grey with white wings and headlamp shields to conform to wartime blackout regulations.

Below and right: Pages from the GWR *Cartage Instruction Book* of 1939, referring to wartime conditions affecting cartage staff.

(643-1)

Page 12, Cartage Instruction Book—Legal Requirements

NATIONAL EMERGENCY LIGHTING REGULATIONS.

Motor Vehicles.

Side Lights, must not show an aperture of more than two inches in diameter which must be obscured with the equivalent of two thicknesses of newspaper. Reflectors must be removed or blackened and no lamp bulb exceeding 7 watts is permitted.

Head lamps, one only is permitted and this must be fitted with approved mask. It is immaterial which lamp is so fitted. No light to show above horizontal. Reflector to be left untouched. Lamp be extinguished immediately on receipt of an air raid warning.

Tail lamp, not to be more than 3' 6" from the ground. Must show red light only and any other light to be blacked out. No lamp bulb exceeding 7 watts is permitted.

Fog lamp, may be used in fog but must be directed down and to the nearside. Police have authority to instruct driver to put out fog lamp at any time.

Horse Vehicles and Trailers (except articulated types) must carry two cart lamps facing forward at a height not greater than 5' 0" from the ground. The upper half of the lamp front glass and the lower half of the reflector must be rendered ineffective. Tail lamps to be carried not more than 3' 6" from ground and must only show red light.

Air Raid Precautions

For the attention of all Carters, Motor Drivers and Vanguards.

FOR THE ATTENTION OF ALL CARTERS.

In the event of a horse vehicle being in the streets when an Air Raid warning is given, or a raid occurs without a warning the Carter is to take the following precautions :—

(1) Return to home station if possible and take horse to stable.

(2) Make use of the nearest Railway premises of any Company.

(3) If there is not sufficient time to do either of the above, horse vehicles must be turned off the main streets and taken into side roads. The best protected site then at hand to be utilised.

(4) Vehicle to be braked and wheels chained.

(5) Horse to be taken out of shafts.

(6) Horse to be secured to rear of vehicle and nosebag put on. Do not remove the bit.

(7) To secure the horse, every animal will wear a stable head collar under the bridle and ropes will be attached to the head collar.

(8) Carters on regular daily rounds should acquaint themselves of suitably protected sites en route where their horse and vehicle could be parked in an emergency.

FOR THE ATTENTION OF ALL MOTOR DRIVERS.

Drivers of motor vehicles should turn into the nearest side street, stop engine, protect load (including driving seat) by tarpaulin cover, and take cover in nearest shelter.

Chapter 5:
Railhead Services

While for the casual sender and consignee the GWR's Country Lorry Service was adequate, it was found that it did not meet the needs of large manufacturers who required a daily service to a multitude of towns and villages at guaranteed dates and times. To meet the requirements of those clients, the Great Western Railway inaugurated, at a large number of stations, what were to become known as 'railhead services'. These were the subject of a special contract with the individual firm concerned, and the facilities available were varied. In most cases, the terms included not only delivery but also collection of empties and the handing of empty credit notes to the firm's customers. A schedule was agreed with the company under which various areas were served on specific days of the week, and the time of arrival at a shop, whether 1 or 20 miles from the railhead, did not appreciably vary from week to week. If the particular firm wished, the GWR vehicles could carry the firm's own livery, and the driver would be supplied with the firm's uniform.

The aim was to supply the type of transport required at a commercial price. In 1928 more than 30 lorries were installed under the agreement, which had commenced in 1923. One important variation of the railhead service was at Cardiff, where delivery was over an extended area at a given flat rate per ton, irrespective of distance, and it was thrown open on the same terms to all firms desiring to avail themselves of it. Biscuits, bacon, tobacco, groceries, etc from London, Liverpool and other distant points destined for the Welsh Valleys were loaded in bulk to Cardiff instead of in small consignments to stations on remote branch lines. They were then delivered to the door of the customer at least a day earlier than was possible with a 'throughout' train service. The difference in cost was slight, but in many cases senders of perishable goods were prepared to pay a somewhat higher charge for the advantage of guaranteed delivery. However, the increased tonnage that was obtained by the railhead service following its inception enabled the GWR to reduce the rate per ton for cartage.

Of course, the main appeal to the trader was cheapness, but he was also influenced by the convenience of being able to get the whole of his deliveries completed over a wide area by one reliable transport agent, with a proper system of mechanical supervision and an adequate supply of relief vehicles.

Below: Railhead distribution in action: a Morris Commercial 2-ton van, Fleet No A2870, delivers goods in the country districts around Cardiff circa 1935.

Above and right: A versatile group of Thornycroft vans and two Burford vehicles (extreme left) stand at Cardiff on 30 July 1930. This array was part of the Co-ordinated Transport Service in the Cardiff area, started by the GWR in 1928. Known as the 'railhead delivery service', the whole responsibility for consignments, including unpacking, collection and crediting of empties etc, was undertaken by the staff at the railhead centre on behalf of the customer. Among the vehicles in the photograph are one or two on contract hire, such as Macfarlane, Lang & Co. This picture was used for the accompanying advertisement which appeared in the GWR Special Centenary Number of the Railway Gazette, 30 August 1935.

RAILHEAD DISTRIBUTION

ALTHOUGH IT IS EARLY MORNING, the RAILHEAD FLEET is ready for the road. Goods received in bulk at the RAILHEADS at BIRMINGHAM, BRISTOL, CARDIFF, EXETER and SWANSEA, have been sorted to the road vehicles for distribution to-day within a radius of 30 miles. The consignments will be placed on the shop shelf and credit notes issued for empties collected.

The RAILHEAD DISTRIBUTION SCHEME places your goods in the most isolated country shops on the day following despatch from the large centres; it achieves economies in packing costs and transport charges by the bulking of small consignments.

Stocks can be maintained in WAREHOUSES on the spot, orders being executed by the Railway Company as required.

Apply to the Chief Goods Manager, Development Department (R.D.), Great Western Railway, Paddington Station, W.2, for a railhead scheme that will suit your requirements.

JAMES MILNE,
General Manager.

Paddington Station,
London, W.2.

Above and left: **Fleet No 2583** is a 2-ton Morris Commercial chassis fitted with a van body especially for railhead services. Photographed at Swindon on 24 September 1932, it is noticeable that the GWR was now satisfied that electric headlamps and sidelamps were fully reliable and there was no provision for oil lamps. Note the different fleet number, 2245, on cabside.

Left: An AEC 3½-ton lorry, Fleet No 411, in trouble in the Bristol area in 1932. Apparently the vehicle was being driven by a learner driver and it hit twin babies in a pram, which was carried across the pavement. The vehicle then went through a fence and down an embankment, which resulted in one baby being killed. It was inevitable that accidents would occur, but considering the number of vehicles operated by the GWR their accident record was low. This lorry appears on page 49 but with a different body.

Right: A close-up of the front of a 30-cwt Thornycroft forward-control lorry, interesting in that it was very unusual for the Thornycroft nameplate to be missing from the radiator. The photograph was taken on 29 January 1932.

Right: Fleet No 2354, a Ford Type B 2-ton chassis fitted with flat platform body No G.1416, was photographed at Bristol Temple Meads circa 1932. Note the different fleet number, 1507, on cabside.

Below: This 2-ton Fordson chassis fitted with a van body, Fleet No 3105, was photographed at Swindon in December 1933. Note that the licence holder shown fixed to the front of the van body had to be refixed to the windscreen during the middle 1930s to conform to new legislation.

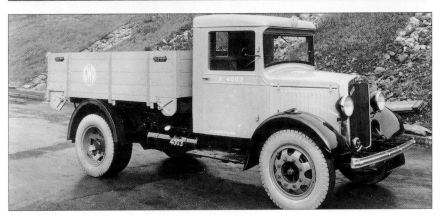

Above: Fleet No 2849, a 2-ton Morris Commercial forward-control chassis fitted with a van body photographed at Swindon on 29 January 1935, is branded for vinegar traffic in connection with Hill, Evans & Co Ltd. On a number of these photographs the original fleet numbers have been altered in ink to show the new numbers to be allocated under a later renumbering scheme. Under the radiator there is a notice telling drivers not to drain the coolant as glycerine had been added.

Left: Fleet No 1512 is a Maudslay ML 3 4/5-ton chassis that has been fitted with a special body for chair traffic, presumably in the High Wycombe area. This vehicle was previously an omnibus and was converted in 1933; it was photographed at Swindon on 21 November of that year.

Left: A 4-ton Morris Commercial 'Leader' chassis fitted with 3cu yd capacity body, No 4003 was photographed in November 1936. The interesting thing about this lorry is the fact that it has a movable floor, the idea being to obtain a more efficient substitute for a tipping vehicle. The floor consisted of a rubber sheet extending across the whole length and width of the lorry and wound over a roller at each end. By the simple operation of winding from one end to the other, a load of sand or similar material could be discharged by hand very quickly. This picture shows the vehicle in what looks like works grey livery; it was probably used departmentally.

Above: No 3174, a Fordson 2-ton chassis fitted with a flat body and detachable sides, was photographed in Swindon Works on 5 September 1934, and shows a couple of points worth noting about its livery. Cast plates of the words 'Great Western Railway' are placed on a cream strip, and the GWR monogram, in use from about August 1934 onwards, is shown here on one of the first road vehicles to bear it.

Centre right: Vehicle No 2826, a Morris Commercial forward-control chassis with a Swindon van body, was photographed at the Works on 15 September 1933.

Right: No 2839 is an almost identical vehicle, except that it has two licence holders in the cab, a requirement necessary under the Road & Rail Traffic Act 1933, as described in the introduction to Chapter 3. This photograph was taken at Swindon Works on 30 November 1934.

Top: In the early 1930s the GWR ordered, for evaluation, two chassis fitted with diesel engines. This photograph, taken at Swindon on 1 February 1934, shows No 2285, a Thornycroft 'Taurus' 6½-ton van with a body built by Swindon. This vehicle had a 28hp four-cylinder compression ignition engine, and the Brockhouse trailer carried a 4½-ton payload; it had a Swindon-built body. Bearing in mind some of the massive vehicles on our roads today, this pair must have looked gigantic in 1934. Note the forward arrangement of bumper bar, which enabled the vehicle to meet legal requirements.

Above: No 3406, a very modern-looking vehicle by any standards, is a 6-ton AEC 'Monarch' chassis with a flat body and fitted with detachable sides built at Swindon; it was photographed at Swindon Works on 26 October 1934. An innovation was the sliding door on the cab; the door handle is very reminiscent of early GWR passenger rolling stock.

Bottom: Vehicle No A3839, a 2-ton Morris Commercial forward-control chassis with a Swindon-built flat body with detachable sides, was photographed at Swindon on 17 February 1938. Vehicles were supplied by the GWR to the GW&GC Joint Committee and bore brown and cream livery.

Above left: **This AEC 3¹/₂-ton platform lorry, Fleet No 426, is loaded with a BX-type container. One wonders if the weight of the container would lift the front wheels off the ground, as it is positioned behind the centre line! The photograph was taken at Paddington in January 1933.**

Above right: **A2770 is a 3-ton Thornycroft 'Nippy' chassis with a flat body fitted with detachable sides. The cab and body were built at Swindon with a sliding door on the offside only. The vehicle was photographed at Swindon Works on 2 June 1939.**

Below: **Fleet No 418, a very dilapidated AEC 3¹/₂-ton lorry, is being loaded with metal ingots by means of an electric magnet at Handsworth on 1 February 1933. The crane is very interesting with an aerial-type mast that has an independent top element to allow rotation. The whole installation was driven by electricity.**

Above: In this picture Fleet No 2267 is a 4-ton PB chassis fitted with platform body G.1967, and is seen at Maidenhead on 24 May 1933 with an immaculate K-type container painted in brown and cream livery complete with coat of arms.

Left: The same vehicle is seen on the same day with the container decorated to take part in the Maidenhead Carnival procession, with a theme intended to advertise household removals. Notice the very nice private-owner wagons of Richard Webster & Sons.

Above: At the beginning of 1934 a new parcels depot was opened at Cardiff, and divided into sections that provided for sorting parcels into their delivery districts. Each van was allocated a district and backed into the appropriate section, and this photograph, taken on 14 February 1934, shows a wonderful line-up of vans. Left to right, they are a 30cwt forward-control Burford, No 823, with solid tyres; a 2-ton Latil (Cie des Automobiles Industrielles Latil) with pneumatic tyres and electric lighting, but no numberplate; two 30cwt Burfords with solid tyres; a 30cwt Thornycroft with full windscreen and pneumatic tyres; a 1-ton Ford with pneumatic tyres; a 1-ton Morris Commercial; and other types.

Below: No 1364 in the GWR fleet and in GWR livery, but on joint GWR and LMS service, this 4-ton Thornycroft forward-control PB chassis with platform body G.1491 is fitted with pneumatic tyres. The LMS H-type 2¼-ton containers were used mainly for fragile earthenware traffic. The photograph was taken in 1934 at Swansea, one of the areas where a joint cartage service operated.

Above and below: **This beautifully turned-out Trojan van was photographed at Alfred Road Garage, Westbourne Park, on 22 April 1936. Of particular note is the easy access through to the driving cab, which must have been a great help when making deliveries. Trojan vehicles will be remembered as they were used in large numbers by Brooke Bond Ltd.**

Above and below: **Fleet No A3864, a 2-ton Morris Commercial forward-control chassis with a half-tilt body and rear-half drop sides, has a paint date of 11 February 1938. The cream-painted tailboard adds a very nice touch.**

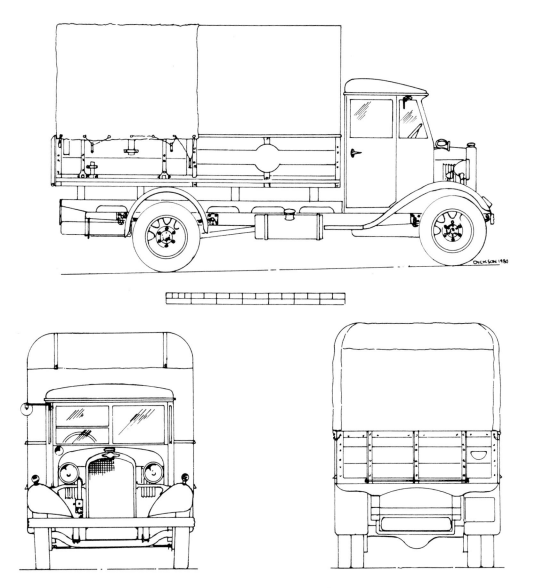

Above: Scale drawing of the 2-ton Morris Commercial. The drawing has been prepared from basic dimensions taken from a weight diagram, and the other details have been estimated from the accompanying photographs.

Below: This 30cwt Scammell lorry, No S4600, is propelled by a 10hp twin-cylinder air-cooled engine situated beneath the body, giving ample clearance for all maintenance purposes and enabling easy access to the cab for the driver. This made his work much easier when delivering many consignments, such as small parcels, to many addresses. Note the collapsible starting handle. A joint effort by Scammell and the Great Western, the lorry is shown here at Slough Road Motor Workshops on 28 January 1938.

Right and centre right: The body of 25/30cwt Morris Commercial van No A4007 was built by the GWR at Swindon; the paint date is 6 December 1938, and the photograph was taken two days later. Although a joint cartage vehicle, the livery was brown and cream, and in order that neither company had preference, the front view shows LMS first, and the rear view GW! The grey panel was provided for current quadroyal posters to be billposted.

Below: A fine line-up of vehicles at Paddington at 3.28pm on 3 November 1938. From right to left they are No 2014, a 30cwt Thornycroft; three Morris Commercials; No B.1089, a Commer; three AECs; a Thornycroft and an Associated Daimler.

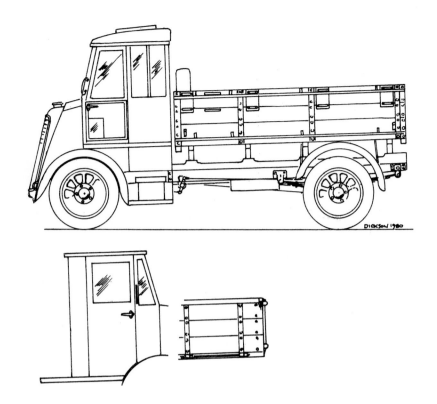

Above: Scale drawing of the 15cwt Commer. The drawing has been prepared from basic dimensions taken from a weight diagram, and the other details have been estimated from the accompanying photographs.

Centre left and left: A524 is a 15cwt Commer fitted with body G.2780, which has hinged sides; the paint date is 19 September 1939 and the photograph was taken at Swindon Works on 7 October 1939. The vehicle is in brown and cream livery together with white wings and masked headlamps to conform with blackout regulations during World War 2.

Right and centre right: **This 3-ton Thornycroft 'Nippy' van No A3205, with a body built at Swindon to Lot 834, was photographed on 21 November 1945. It has a sliding door fitted to the offside only. These vehicles proved to be a very efficient addition to the fleet and gave good service.**

EXPRESS
CARTAGE
SERVICES

A3205

GYH 35

EXPRESS
CARTAGE
SERVICES

Below: **Another 3-ton Thornycroft 'Nippy', Fleet No A3180, has a platform body and is collecting merchandise at Sulhampstead Abbots on 18 November 1946. Notice the completely different cab from that shown above.**

GYH 74

Above: Fleet No A3180 is seen again, but this time making deliveries later in the day at Theale.

Below: Two 4-ton Thornycroft vehicles in a very picturesque setting, both fitted with flat bodies carrying 4-ton-capacity containers. It is interesting to note that the right-hand lorry, registration No GC 9156, also appears on page 95 fitted with sides for gravel haulage. This photograph was taken at Wexcombe Manor near Marlborough on 30 September 1937 during a household removal – another facet of the Great Western Cartage Department.

Above: During 1940 the GWR was asked to move various schools that had been evacuated at the outbreak of war in 1939 back to their normal sites. One such was Malvern College, whose 140 tons of effects needed to be moved from its temporary quarters at Blenheim Palace back to Malvern, with delivery required to 25 different addresses. In all, 76 vehicles were collected together from adjacent stations to carry out the exercise, and many different types were used, including containers. An idea of this can be obtained from the photograph taken at Blenheim Palace on 1 August 1940. On the extreme left is 2-ton Thornycroft No A2553, with utility body and trailer, normally used for farm traffic; next is A2640, a 2-ton Thornycroft 'Trusty' flat with removable sides; and at the rear is a 4-ton Thornycroft cattle van.

Below: Another similar removal involved Shrewsbury School. This photograph was taken on 4 April 1940 and shows a 2-ton Thornycroft 'Handy' with a utility body. On the cabside is the GWR monogram, but the bodyside bears three cast plates: 'GW&/LMS/RLY's'.

Above left: **As seen earlier during World War 1, experiments were again made during the 1939-45 conflict with alternative fuels. The 2-ton Morris Commercial parcel van shown here is running on coal gas in July 1940. The bag was restrained in a collapsible steel frame that expanded after filling and had a capacity of about 350cu ft – 250cu ft was approximately equivalent to 1 gallon of petrol. It will be seen that the contents of the bag is equal to $1^2/_5$ gallons of petrol. On delivery work this covers about half a day's work so that it is necessary to fill up twice daily, at a suitable filling point, through a 2in-diameter pipe. Very little alteration was necessary to the engine other than fitting a gas carburettor and a change-over valve to enable the vehicle to be run on petrol if required.**

Top right: **As can be seen from these next two pictures, life wasn't always dull in the Road Motor Department. This 4-ton Thornycroft vehicle, seen at Bristol Temple Meads repair shops, was apparently near the runway at Yeovil airfield in 1943 when it was hit by a landing aircraft that sliced through the cab. It was reported that the driver and his mate were uninjured.**

Left: **Having run out of control on the Portway between Bristol and Avonmouth on 19 January 1945, AEC 'Monarch' 6-ton platform lorry No B8179 is loaded, or almost loaded, with two LMS A-type containers. The lorry was badly damaged and brought back to Bristol Temple Meads repair shop in $1^1/_2$ hours, which was good teamwork by staff. It was soon repaired and put back into service.**

Right and below: Fleet No A4601 is a 30cwt Scammell *rigid* three-wheel chassis fitted with flat body G.2674. The paint date is 4 May 1938, and it was photographed at Swindon on 30 May 1938.

Below and below right: The rear wheels of Fleet No S4623, a Fordson 'Sussex' six-wheeler fitted with a 14-foot body, are fitted with special tyres, no doubt for use over rough terrain, while the body, G.2738, has a timber support at the front end to carry long loads. The individual planks making up the sides are stamped with the body number, as was done with locomotive side-rods etc. The photograph was taken at Swindon on 28 January 1939.

Left and below: **Fleet No A4055 is a 2-ton Morris Commercial 'Equi-Load' van produced for the Signal Department, Neath, and was photographed at Swindon on 28 January 1939.**

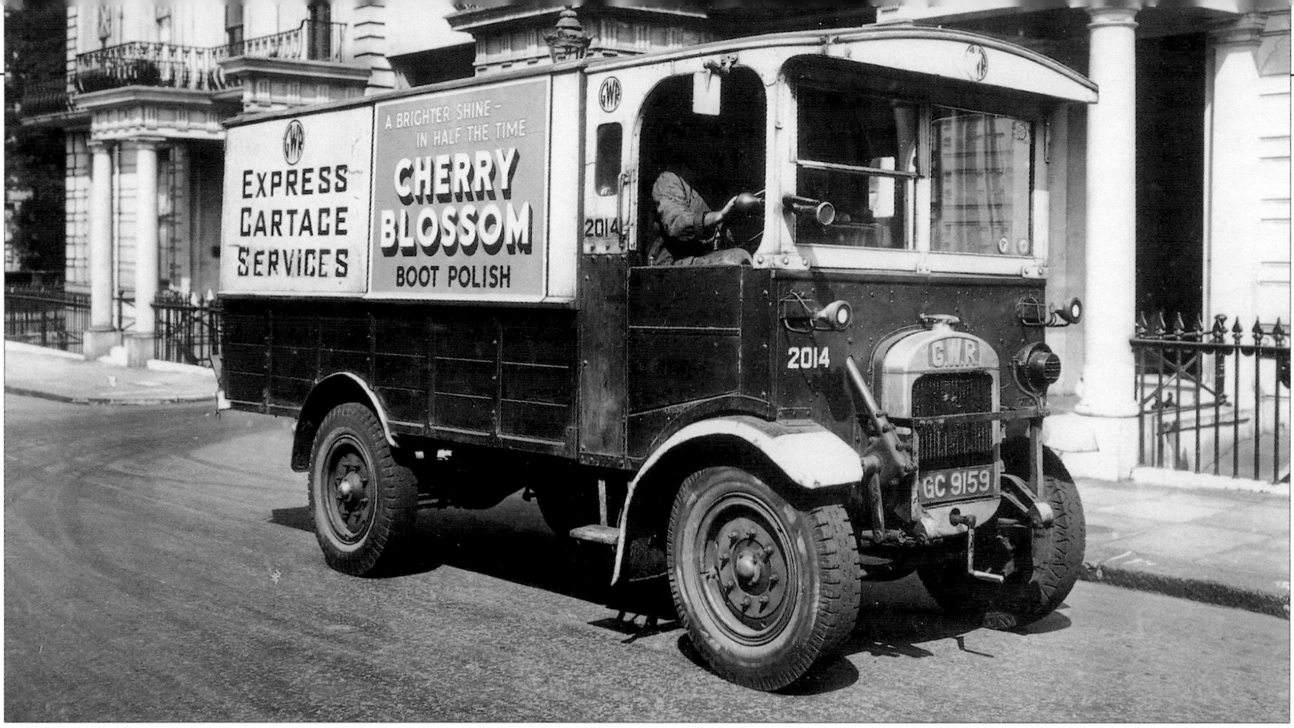

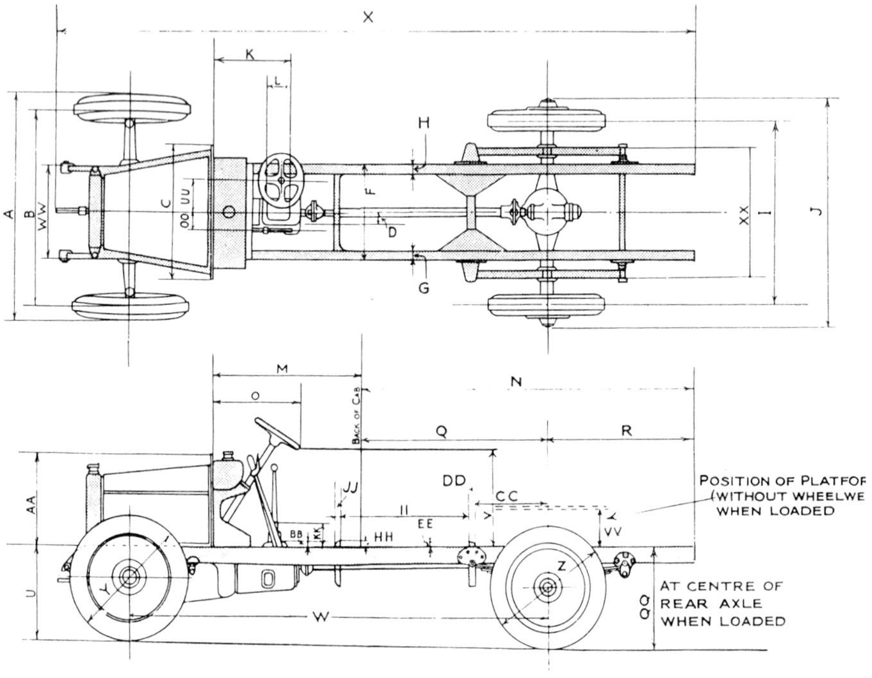

Above: Fleet No 2014, a 30cwt forward-control Thornycroft A1 chassis with a Swindon-built body, was photographed at Orsett Terrace, Paddington, on 2 July 1940. The wings are whitened and the headlamp masked for blackout conditions, as described previously.

Left: Dimensions of the A1 chassis for use by body builders.

Right and bottom right: Karrier 'Bantam' 2-ton van, Fleet No A2813, was photographed at Swindon Works on 16 February 1945. The standard livery has the usual blackout additions – notice the headlamp low down on the nearside and the very modern typeface for the lettering.

Body Builders' Diagrams of THORNYCROFT Type "A1" Freight Chas

DIMENSIONS.

On standard 36 ins. × 6 ins. Dunlop pneumatic tyres

		ft.	ins.	metres.			ft.	ins.	metres.			ft.	ins.	metres.			ft.	ins.	me
A	...	5	11¾	1·822	L	...		8¼	·210	Y	...	3	2¼	·972	HH	...		1½	·
B	...	5	1⅝	1·565	M	...	4	1	1·245	*Y	...	3	0¼	·921	II	...	3	7¾	1·
†B	...	4	10⅝	1·514	N	...	10	0	3·048	†Y	...	3	0	·914	JJ	...		2	·
C	...	3	6	1·067	O	...	2	5	·737	Z	...	3	2¼	·972	KK	...		7½	·
D	...		4	·102	Q	...	5	3	1·600	*Z	...	3	0¼	·921	OO	...		5	·
F	...	2	6½	·775	R	...	4	9	1·448	†Z	...	3	0	·914	QQ	...	2	7	·
G	...		3	·076	U	...	2	5	·737	AA	...	2	4⅞	·733	*QQ	...	2	6	·
H	...		3	·076	*U	...	2	4	·711	BB	...		1¼	·032	UU	...		10¼	·
I	...	5	0⅞	1·546	V	...	2	5¼	·743	CC	...	2	0	·610	VV	...	1	0	·
†I	...	4	10⅞	1·495	W	...	11	6	3·505	DD	...		2	·051	WW	...	2	8	·
J	...	5	11½	1·816	X	...	18	1¼	5·518	EE	...		1½	·038	XX	...	3	7	1·
K	...	2	1	·635															

* Varying dimensions for alternative 34 ins. × 7 ins. Dunlop pneumatic tyres.

† Varying dimensions for alternative 36 ins. × 3½ ins. resilient solid tyres.

The above dimensions are subject to alteration, and should be confirmed by us before bodywork is commence

For Prices, Terms of Business and Guarantee, see Price List.

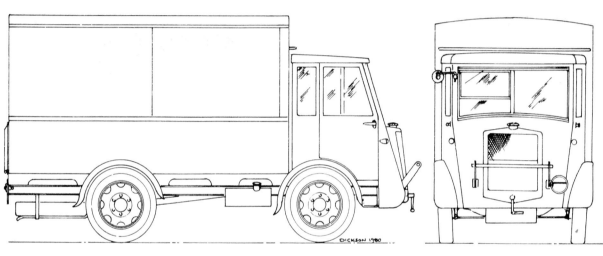

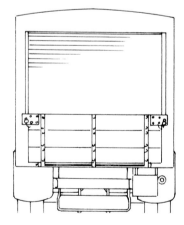

Above: Scale drawing of the 2-ton Karrier. The drawing has been prepared from basic dimensions taken from a weight diagram, and the other details have been estimated from the accompanying photographs.

Right: Fleet No 2493 is a Thornycroft BE/FB4 'Handy' chassis fitted with 11-foot flat body No G.2127, with removable sides and hoops. It was photographed at Swindon on 17 January 1934. Notice the different fleet number.

Right: Another Thornycroft, this time a BE 'Trusty' chassis, Fleet No A3231, has been fitted with half-tilt body No G.2470. It was in 1933 that Thornycroft began to adopt class names for its vehicles; the 'Handy' came out in 1933, the 'Trusty' in 1934, the 'Sturdy' in 1935, and the 'Nippy' in 1937. This example was photographed at Swindon on 12 May 1936. Notice the different fleet number.

Left: This 'Trusty' chassis, Fleet No S2936, has been fitted with a special cab and a 17-foot flat body, designed to carry long loads on the body and beside the cab. It was photographed at Swindon on 16 April 1937. Notice the different fleet number.

Left: Fleet No B5008 is a Thornycroft 5-ton 'Sturdy' chassis with flat body G.2974 with tailboards and detachable sides. Photographed at Swindon on 17 March 1945, again it bears the wartime white wings and masked headlamps.

Centre left: This six-wheeler, Fleet No S9012, is a Dennis 'Jubilant' chassis fitted with body G.3303, which had hinged sides. The engine was a six-cylinder diesel, and it is understood that the vehicle could carry up to 12 tons. It was photographed shortly after delivery to the GWR in 1946.

Below: This Dennis 'Jubilant', Fleet No S9016, has been fitted with platform body G.3307, and has specially adapted steel and timber trestles in order to carry such long and heavy loads. It is seen in the Birmingham area in 1947.

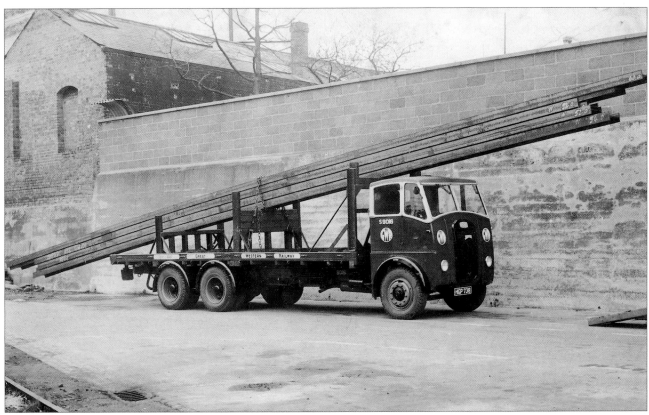

This page: **Built for the GWR by Douglas (Kingswood) Limited of Bristol, these 2-ton electric parcels vans were fitted with 258 amp/hour Exide 'Ironclad' batteries. Special modifications were made at the request of the GWR, which consisted of tailboard, roller shutter at the rear, and a floor with corrugated aluminium and oak inserts. No E2801 was used in the Bristol area for express parcels services and both were photographed in 1947 shortly after delivery from the manufacturer.**

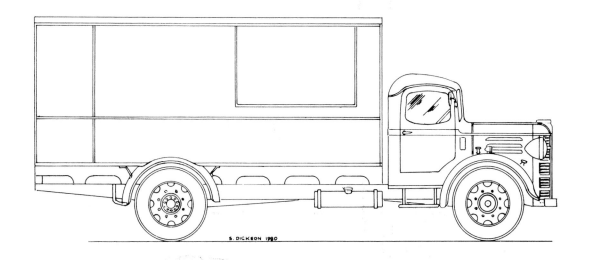

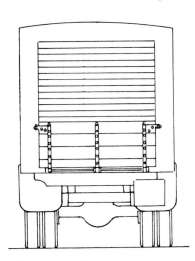

Top: Scale drawing of the 2-ton Austin. The drawing has been prepared from basic dimensions taken from a weight diagram, and the other details have been estimated from the accompanying photograph.

Centre right: Photographed circa 1946 is a Vulcan 6VF chassis with a 5-ton flat body; the fleet number is B5058 and the body G.3159.

Below: Eight days after nationalisation, the Great Western sets up a road block! This very clean 2-ton Austin van was posed for photography especially to capture the Churchman's cigarette advert. The livery is the usual brown and cream, and it appears that the tyre walls are painted brick red, which was fashionable for a time. The photograph was taken near Paddington on 8 January 1948.

Repair and Maintenance

Below: The GWR purchased All Saints' Church in Tyndall Street, Cardiff, in 1901, and it was used in turn as a power house, an oil store and a biscuit warehouse. In 1929 the Road Transport Department took it over for use as a repair shop and garage, and what had been the vestry became the Foreman's office and stores. The altar area became an inspection pit, and instead of seating 400 people the building accommodated 12 motor lorries and associated workshop equipment. One hopes that all repairs were carried out very religiously and not left to providence! These photographs were taken on 14 May 1936 – note the tyre that has been moved during the exposure.

Above: During April 1920 the GWR started the construction of a motor vehicle garage and workshop at Alfred Road, Westbourne Park, in West London. It consisted of three bays, overhauling, machine shops and stores, while a separate building contained offices, kitchens and messrooms. The floor space of the bays was 188 feet by 143ft 6in. This photograph of the interior was taken on 10 July 1934. This garage was demolished some time ago and the site is now covered by a concrete viaduct carrying the 'Westway' link to the A40.

Below: This photograph of Alfred Road Garage shows a detail of part of the Machine Shop with vertical drilling machines and lathes. Note the two Morris Commercial forward-control vehicles with consecutive registration numbers. The date of the photograph is 16 January 1933.

Above and below: A glorious collection of vehicles – AEC, Thornycroft, Burford, Morris Commercial and Associated Daimler – can all be seen in this general view inside Alfred Road Garage on 6 January 1933. The Austin car in the foreground is having rather more than a 6,000-mile service, and is thought to be that of the Road Motor Engineer – it is surprising that a gasket should be placed on the rear upholstery. It is all a bit reminiscent of Swindon 'A' Shop!

Above: Two Associated Daimler lorries and one Thornycroft are undergoing maintenance in the Alfred Road Depot on 6 January 1933. The Thornycroft, Fleet No 1363, is a 4-ton forward-control PB chassis with body G.546 with sides and tilt. The two Associated Daimlers, Nos 1919 and 1913, are 4/5-ton chassis, one with a van body and the other with a platform body. Notice the tiled pit and very gloomy conditions within the depot.

Below: Outside Alfred Road Garage on 10 July 1934 the van on the left is a 4-ton Thornycroft forward-control PB chassis fitted with a high-sided body. No 2741 is a 3-ton Scammell 'mechanical horse' with trailer T.235, and is taking on fuel. On the right 4/5-ton Associated Daimler No 1922 shows its rear end, and finally there is horse-drawn wagon No 2251. An interesting sign on the boom of the fuel pump reads 'Remember, no racing on a cold engine – DON'T FORGET YOUR PETROL BONUS!' At this time the drivers were paid an extra allowance if they saved petrol.

Chapter 6:
The Zonal Goods Organisation

One of the last ideas of the GWR in October 1947, before it became extinct as a result of nationalisation, was the finalisation of the Zonal Goods Organisation. The railway system was divided into 36 zones to improve transit of 'smalls' traffic by concentration of handling and by motor services. The first zonal collection and delivery scheme for miscellaneous goods traffic was introduced in Birmingham during December 1945.

The purpose of zoning was to provide overnight delivery of small consignments between any two stations, even in rural areas. It was achieved by concentrating the handling of traffic at a reduced number of stations, thereby increasing the possibility of forwarding points being able to make up full wagon loads for through transit to a destination, known as sub-railhead or railhead, from which there was a direct road delivery service to the consignee. Combined with this was the extended use of road transport for the wider collection and distribution of traffic in areas that were not served previously, and the substitution of motor transport for short-distance rail haulage.

When direct transit to a sub-railhead was impracticable, traffic was sent to the railhead station in the same zone as the sub-railhead serving the destination. It then completed its journey by a trunk motor service to the sub-railhead, and thence by direct delivery motor to the consignee. Every zone was therefore based on a railhead, which operated direct delivery services in its own vicinity and also trunk motors to a number of sub-railheads. The railheads were situated at important towns or traffic centres, and the aim in operating the scheme was to bypass them as much as possible by sending traffic direct between sub-railheads, except when transfer was unavoidable.

The trunk motor schedules from the railheads ensured that consignments loaded to them for a sub-railhead were forwarded as soon as possible after receipt, instead of waiting for an overnight railway wagon. Every railhead had its own direct delivery area from which it received, and to which it delivered, traffic by road motor. Trunk motors operated on fixed schedules between railhead and sub-railheads; they did not collect or deliver en route, that work being left to the direct delivery motors radiating from the sub-railheads.

The type of vehicle used for trunk or local delivery services varied according to the locality. The type found most useful for the class of work was the 6/8-ton or 3-ton four-wheeled articulated lorry and trailer. In some districts it was found that a 5/6-ton rigid vehicle was suitable for trunk service operation, particularly as such a vehicle had a speed limit of 30mph as against the 20mph of a 6/8-ton articulated lorry.

Below: **Vehicles ready to leave Tyseley sub-railhead in the Birmingham zone, on their morning rounds.**

Above: The Vulcan 5/6-ton lorry was a type of vehicle found suitable for the operation of trunk services in certain districts.

Below: Area covered by the Worcester zone, showing the long trips undertaken by direct delivery vehicles.

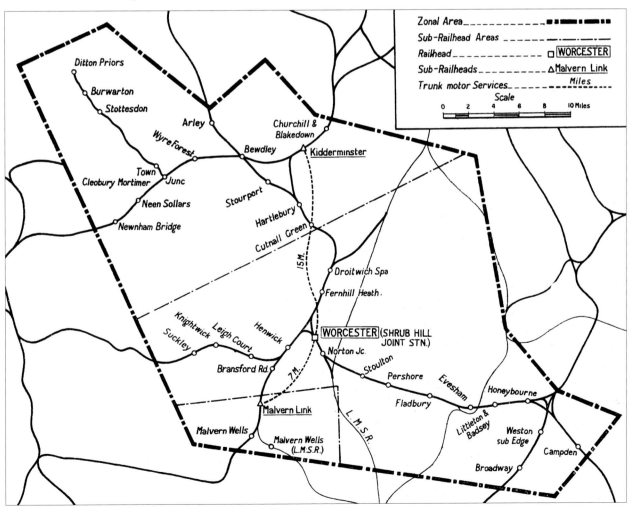

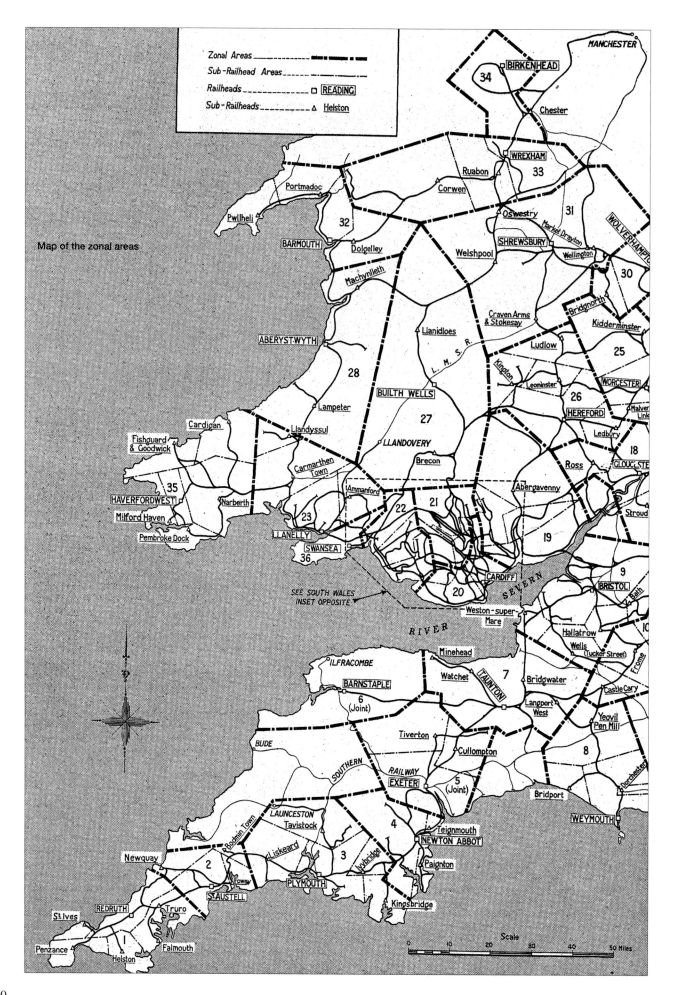

Map of the zonal areas

Zonal Areas _____
Sub-Railhead Areas _____
Railheads _____ □ READING
Sub-Railheads _____ △ Helston

MANCHESTER
BIRKENHEAD
34
Chester
WREXHAM
Ruabon
33
Corwen
Oswestry
31
Portmadoc
Market Drayton
WOLVERHAMPTON
Pwllheli
32
SHREWSBURY
Wellington
BARMOUTH
Dolgelley
Welshpool
30
Machynlleth
Bridgnorth
Craven Arms & Stokesay
Kidderminster
Llanidloes
Ludlow
25
ABERYSTWYTH
L.M.S.R.
Kington
Leominster
WORCESTER
28
Malvern Link
BUILTH WELLS
26
Lampeter
HEREFORD
27
Ledbury
Cardigan
Llandyssul
LLANDOVERY
18
Fishguard & Goodwick
Brecon
Ross
Carmarthen Town
GLOUCESTER
35
Ammanford
Abergavenny
Narberth
22
21
Stroud
HAVERFORDWEST
23
19
Milford Haven
LLANELLY
9
Pembroke Dock
SWANSEA
CARDIFF
BRISTOL
36
20
Bath
SEE SOUTH WALES INSET OPPOSITE
Weston-super-Mare
SEVERN
RIVER
Hallatrow
10
Wells (Tucker Street)
Minehead
Frome
ILFRACOMBE
Watchet
7
Bridgwater
BARNSTAPLE
TAUNTON
Castle Cary
6 (Joint)
Langport West
Yeovil Pen Mill
Tiverton
8
BUDE
Cullompton
Dorchester
SOUTHERN RAILWAY
5 (Joint)
Bridport
EXETER
LAUNCESTON
4
WEYMOUTH
Tavistock
Teignmouth
NEWTON ABBOT
Newquay
3
Ivybridge
Paignton
Bodmin Town
Liskeard
2
PLYMOUTH
Kingsbridge
Fowey
S.AUSTELL
REDRUTH
Truro
St Ives
1
Penzance
Helston
Falmouth

Scale
0   10   20   30   40   50 Miles

140

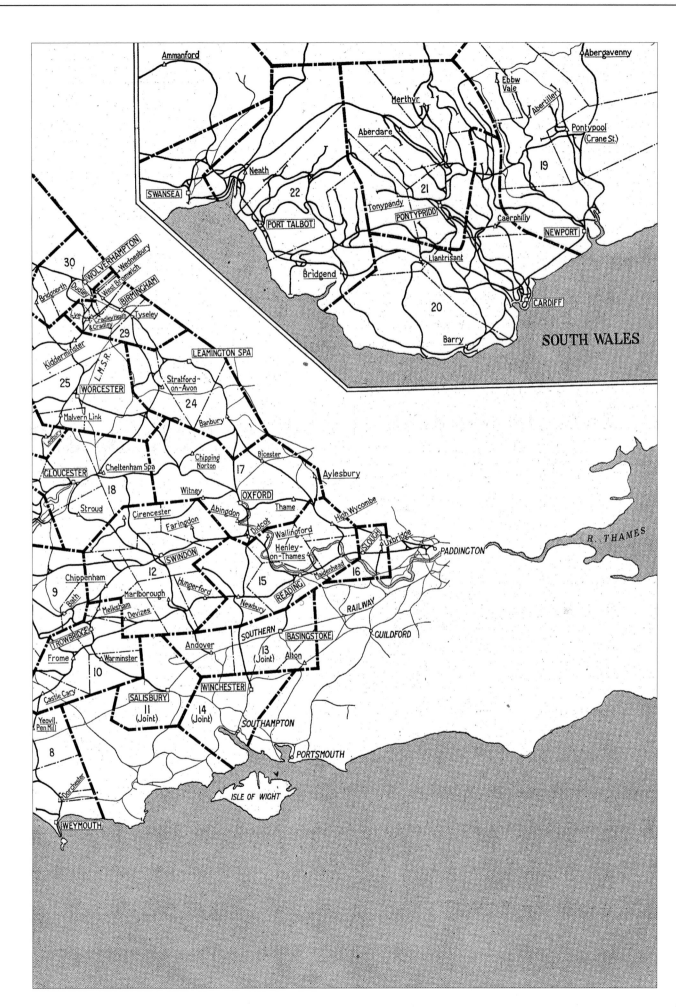

SOUTH WALES

Above: Loading wagons by perambulation direct from the collection vehicle.

Below: The goods shed at Dudley was altered to provide additional berthing space for zone scheme road vehicles, and other improvements.

Chapter 7:
Mechanical Horses, Tractors and Trailers

The horse was considered economically indispensable for short-distance haulage work, particularly in congested areas, and while the motor vehicle gradually displaced the horse in many spheres of operation, a vehicle of a special design was necessary to equal the horse-drawn vehicle in every respect. These properties were incorporated in the mechanically propelled articulated lorry, resulting in higher speed and greater carrying capacity, both attributes materially assisting in reducing street congestion. The trailer portion was easily detachable, and the whole operation of coupling was almost automatic, necessitating only the reversal of the tractor to the trailer – the design of the coupling gear enabled the lorry to be coupled without the driver leaving his cab. This 'mechanical horse' and trailer made for extreme ease of manoeuvring – the turning circle was no greater than that of a horse vehicle, and considerably less than the conventional motor vehicle.

It is interesting to note that in 1934 an agreement was made between the four main-line railway companies and Scammell Lorries Limited concerning the Scammell Patent Coupling Gear. It was agreed that the gear could be used by the railway companies on vehicles other than those built by Scammell, and also the coupling gear could be manufactured by the railway companies on payment of certain royalties.

Below: **As previously stated, experiments were started in 1931 with three-wheel motor tractors towing horse-drawn vehicles for short distances only. This photograph of Fleet No 2702 during a demonstration at South Lambeth Goods Depot was taken on 16 September 1931 and shows a Karrier 'Cob' tractor fitted with a 9hp petrol engine and 'Henley Air Cushion' solid tyres. Behind it the former horse-drawn lorry has been adapted as a trailer with special wheels and an elementary coupling system.**

Above: This photograph shows another Karrier 'Cob', Fleet No 2700, again demon-strating at South Lambeth on 16 September 1931, this time with unadapted horse-drawn wagon No 370 – a genuine mechanical horse-drawn vehicle that doesn't need feeding!

Right: Another view of Karrier 'Cob' No 2700 with an adapted ex-motor lorry chassis. Notice the empty housing that held the differential gear.

Right: Fleet No 2714, another Karrier 'Cob' three-wheel tractor, is coupled to articulated trailer T.187 fitted with special high sides at Swindon on 1 November 1932. Notice the horse 'mascot' on the bonnet.

Left: Another 'Cob', Fleet No 2725, is seen with articulated van body No T.194 at Swindon on 21 January 1933.

Below: Owing to the increase in the company's cartage and the greater diversity in the loads carried, different types of road vehicles were required. At the end of 1929 there were 287 motor units in service, and the vehicles shown here are a pair of 10-ton tractors, Fleet Nos 1082 and 1080, built by Scammell Lorries Ltd of Watford, with permanently coupled trailers fitted with high sides, at the premises of the St Martin Preserving Co Ltd, Slough Trading Estate, on 23 September 1929. Did the sacks carry manufactured pips for the raspberry jam?

Bottom: A close-up of Fleet No 1080 on the same day. Note the jackshaft just below the rear of the cab – this terminated in a sprocket wheel interchangeable with another size to give a different gear ratio if required. Today a 10-speed gearbox is used.

Above: Fleet No 1086 is a Leyland six-wheeled lorry that appears to conform to the same configuration as the Scammells opposite. It bears a paint date of May 1930.

Right and below: During 1935 the GWR, in conjunction with the LMS, purchased the livestock haulage business of Smith Bros at Knowle. Fleet No C2538 is one of the 3-ton short-wheelbase Morris Commercial tractors fitted with a Tasker cattle van trailer taken over from Smith Bros. It is shown here at Swindon Works after renovation in July 1935. Of interest is the one-piece windscreen, wiper and electric horn. The tractor had normal GWR livery but the trailer was varnished wood with black ironwork. The second photograph shows the rear view of a similar vehicle, photographed at Swindon on 26 October 1935.

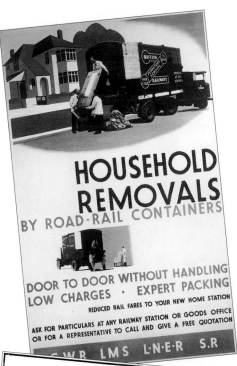

Left: Posters issued to advertise household removals. The artwork was produced from some of the following photographs.

Above: Cartoon reproduced from *Great Western Railway Magazine.*

Below: As mentioned previously, the arrival of the 'mechanical horse' and trailer brought a revolution in the cartage business. Up to 1935 the practice of replacing horses by motor vehicles was followed as the occasion appeared justified, but from then on a policy of completely motorising certain stations was started. Two types of articulated vehicles were available, of 3 and 6 tons, with tractors of 10hp and 14hp respectively, and these were admirable for the purpose. With the comparatively small expense of the bodies it was possible for one motor unit to be employed on an unlimited variety of traffic, and it could be attached or detached at a moment's notice. Here a 6-ton Scammell three-wheel tractor, Fleet No C.3900, with a Dyak G trailer complete with 4-ton-capacity container undertakes a typical house removal job at Hanwell on 20 November 1936. 'Dyak' was a telegraphic code name, similar to that used for rail wagons.

Above and below: Two further views of the same tractor and trailer at Hanwell on 20 November 1936. The trailer could be left and the container unloaded while the tractor went off to another job.

Above: Photographed at Warwick Avenue near Paddington in 1937, this 3-ton Scammell three-wheel tractor, No C3621, has Dyak K trailer No T.1373 fitted with a Swindon-built half-tilt body. Note that the tarpaulin is allocated to the vehicle in question and bears the monogram and trailer number.

Left: This 6-ton Scammell three-wheel tractor, Fleet No 2737, has a platform trailer complete with sheeted load. Note the larger cab and headlight.

Below: Dimensional drawing of a 6-ton Scammell 'mechanical horse' with a flat platform body.

Scale: 4mm/ft.

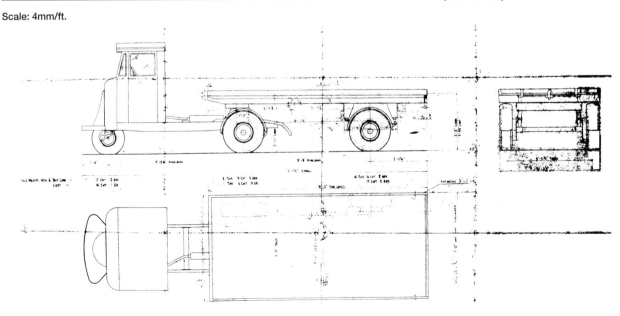

149

Above: No 2735, a typical 3-ton 'mechanical horse' and trailer built by Scammell Lorries of Watford, photographed in mid-1930s near the firm's factory. The tractor was powered by a 10hp engine, while the trailer was fitted with detachable sides and ends. Note that there are no cab doors.

Below: Another vehicle of the same type, but in this instance built for the GW&GCJR and finished in LNER dark blue livery. The fleet number is J.19.

Left: A larger version of the 'Cob' type built by Karrier Motors Ltd, Huddersfield, Fleet No C 4104 is a 3-ton three-wheeled tractor. The 'Cobs', named after the strong short-legged horse, were used alongside the Scammells. This photograph was taken at Swindon on 23 February 1937; with the advent of panchromatic film it is easier to tell the difference between brown and black. Notice that the small horse on the bonnet has gone, replaced by a normal radiator filler cap.

Left: Dyak U 3-ton Scammell trailer No T.1167 is fitted with a Swindon half-tilt body. The paint date is 27 October 1936, and it was photographed two days later at Swindon.

Below left: This 3-ton Scammell trailer, No T3042, is painted in GWR colours for the LMS and GW Railways joint cartage services. The paint date is 22 October 1934, and the photograph was taken at Swindon on 20 December 1934.

Below: Six-ton Scammell trailer No T.431 is fitted with hinged sides and additional slotted-in slats. Again, the paint date is 22 October 1934, photographed at Swindon on 20 December 1934. The skeleton trailers were delivered to Swindon, which decided on the type of body required and built it.

Above: Two views of a 6-ton Scammell trailer with a Swindon-built half-tilt body, type Dyak OJ No T.1783. It was photographed at Swindon Works on 21 June 1938.

Below: Front and rear views of 6-ton Scammell three-wheel tractor Fleet No C6289 at Swindon Works after emerging from the paint shop; the paint date is 26 January 1940, and it was photographed on the 28th. The masked headlamp and white-edged mudguards and bumper comply with blackout regulations during World War 2.

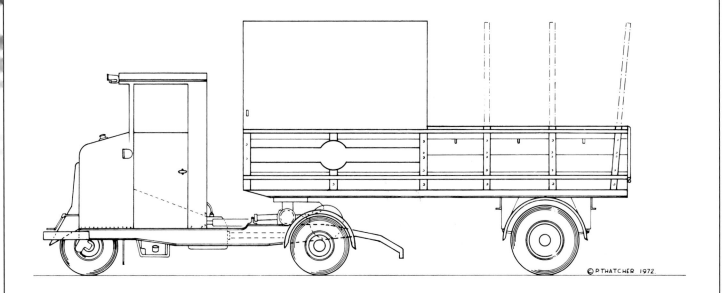

Scale 7mm/1ft

© P. THATCHER 1972.

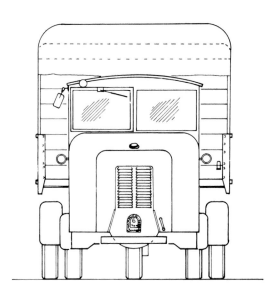

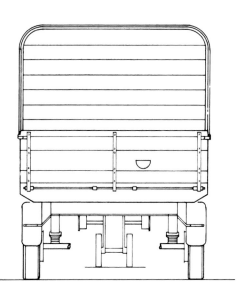

Above: **Scale drawing of the Scammell 6-ton tractor and Dyak OF trailer.**

Above: This is 6-ton trailer No T.1267 built by Messrs Crane and fitted with a Scammell coupling. Designated type Dyak G by the GWR, it is shown here after being painted in standard livery on 15 April 1937.

Below: This 3-ton Scammell trailer with Swindon body No T.1679 was designated type Dyak OH. The paint date is 22 August 1938, and the photograph was taken shortly after.

Above: The Dyak P was a 6-ton Scammell drop-frame trailer. No T.994 was photographed at Swindon on 12 May 1936.

Left: Coded Dyak S, this 6-ton Tasker drop-frame trailer is fitted with high sides, hoop-sticks and tarpaulin. No T.1804 was photographed at Swindon on 15 September 1938.

Below: Six-ton Scammell trailer No T.1848, code Dyak G, is fitted with a special body for Messrs Spiller's traffic. It was photographed at Swindon on 3 October 1939.

Below left: No T.1381 is a 3-ton Scammell AL trailer fitted with a half-tilt body with fixed sides. This Dyak K was photographed at Swindon on 4 February 1938.

Above: Thornycroft 'Nippy' four-wheeled tractor No S8816, with a haulage capacity of 8 tons. The Swindon-built cab with sliding doors is very similar to that on vehicle No A2770 seen on page 114. It had the same coupling as the three-wheeled type. The paint date is 25 July 1940, and the white-edged wings were required by wartime blackout regulations.

Below: A 3-ton Karrier 'Cob' and two 3/6-ton Scammell tractors with Dyak F trailers are distributing Anderson shelter parts from Westbourne Park yard in April 1939 prior to the outbreak of World War 2. Note that there are three licence holders in cab, including one for the trailer.

Left, centre left and below: Two views of a 6-ton Morris Commercial tractor, Fleet No S2530, seen here coupled to a special Hooper trailer fitted with the patent movable floor (below) manufactured by the Principality Wagon Co Ltd of Cardiff. As can be seen, a load could be dropped at the back, then wound forward to the front or vice versa. The photographs were taken in November 1936.

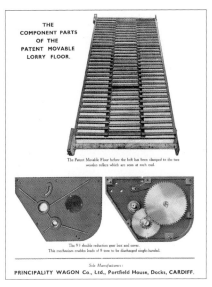

THE COMPONENT PARTS OF THE PATENT MOVABLE LORRY FLOOR.

The Patent Movable Floor before the belt has been clamped to the two wooden rollers which are seen at each end.

The 9 1 double reduction gear box and cover. This mechanism enables loads of 8 tons to be discharged single-handed.

Sole Manufacturers:

PRINCIPALITY WAGON Co., Ltd., Portfield House, Docks, CARDIFF.

Below: Fleet No C4020 is a Morris Commercial four-wheel tractor with a special trailer that also has the Principality floor. The trailer, numbered T.1611, appears to be grey, and was photographed at Slough in October 1937.

Above: Fleet No S8805 is a Thornycroft 'Nippy' four-wheeled tractor with 8-ton Scammell trailer No T.1837, a Dyak OO. It was photographed at Swindon on 3 October 1939.

Right and below: Pictured at Hockley Basin on 22 August 1944 is No D8890, a Bedford Scammell 6/8-ton tractor. Bedfords of this type were supplied to the Army as conventional lorries and were well known throughout the country. This vehicle has the standard Scammell coupling gear for hauling trailers, and is shown with the usual blackout additions.

Above: A Thornycroft 'Nippy' four-wheeled tractor, No D8852, is seen here hauling low-loader trailer No 7550, which is fitted with a cattle-type container. It was photographed outside Newberys Limited, Reading, on 1 April 1946.

Below: On 3 June 1947 the GWR Goods Department arranged an exhibition at St Ervans Road Depot, Westbourne Park, London, showing vehicles, mechanised handling equipment and containers, etc. One such exhibit is shown here, Foden four-wheeled tractor No S482, together with Dyson Titan C low-loader trailer No T.2002.

Above: Bedford Scammell four-wheeled tractor No C8934 is coupled to a Jason F Hydraulic tipping trailer No T.7808, photographed at the same exhibition as on the previous page. It is noticeable that nearly all the vehicles were purchased complete from the manufacturers at this time.

Below: Foden tractor No S481 is coupled to special Titan D trailer No T.1121 and is still in GWR livery two years after nationalisation. The trailer is fitted with eight pairs of wheels and was photographed at Usk on 5 January 1950 while offloading rail-to-road polymer containers that had come from British Nylon Spinners at Billingham.

Left: In 1918 the GWR carried out experiments with the use of a combination motor lorry, which consisted of a tractor with a powerful internal combustion engine working in conjunction with two-wheeled semi-trailers. The 'Knox' tractor was imported from the USA, while the adapted trailer was built partly at Swindon and partly at Slough, and was fitted with hinged legs.

Centre left: In 1922 trials were carried out with an adapted Fordson tractor, supplied by Messrs A. & S. Andrews Ltd, Ealing Common, London, which took the place of the more usual horse. The tractor was attached to an ordinary horse lorry and worked between Paddington and Victoria & Albert Docks, a distance of 14 miles, the idea being to devise a means of reducing the detention of an ordinary motor vehicle while being loaded or unloaded. This photograph was taken on 22 June 1922.

Below: Another picture of horse-drawn lorry No 2116, but this time drawn by Fordson tractor No 390. In this photograph, taken in July 1925, a shorter shaft is being used and the load is sheeted. Note different livery.

Above: Yet another system was demonstrated at Paddington in June 1925, and this time an AEC 3½-ton chassis, Fleet No 422, was used with the Rendell demountable system for transferring the load from the lorry to an adapted horse-drawn trailer, in this case No 1910.

Right: Owing to the increase in the carriage of cable drums, pipes and sugar beet, more tractors were required for hauling the special trailers. This picture shows a Fordson tractor with an Eagle trailer at Bampton on 26 October 1926. The rear wheels bear the initials M-H, this item having been supplied by Muir-Hill (E. Boydell & Co Ltd of Old Trafford).

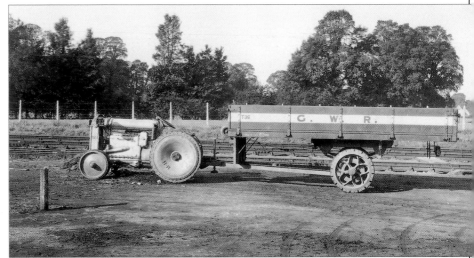

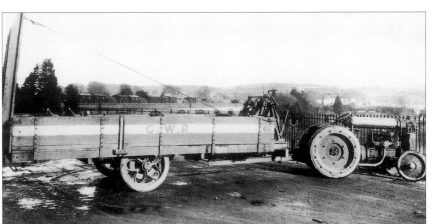

Right: Another Fordson tractor with an Eagle trailer, specially adapted to carry cable drums and photographed in 1937.

Left: This Fordson tractor has a trailer adapted for the conveyance of sugar beet, photographed in 1927. The amount of beet carried in that year was 10,000 tons.

Centre left: A tractor built by McCormick-Deering Co, Rock Island, Illinois, USA, is hauling a trailer with a 20-ton load, also in 1927. When this photograph was taken, this tractor was the only one of its type in Great Britain used for cartage work.

Above and below: On 15 March 1929 a Fordson tractor with no fleet number is shown fitted with sprung rear wheels supplied by Muir-Hill, as previously mentioned.

Above and below: No, this isn't the Western Front in 1915, but the installation of the Swindon water pipeline on 15 June 1928, in which the GWR was closely involved. The picture shows how the pipes were transported in wet weather: a GWR Fordson tractor fitted with chains hauls a trailer constructed from two wagon wheels.

Above and below: **Fordson tractors are hauling converted horse-drawn floats at Torre in connection with the Bath & West and Southern Counties Show held at Torquay on 27 May 1930. Some idea of the business that devolved upon the GWR can be gained from the fact that 383 wagons of general exhibits were received and 423 wagons despatched; 298 wagons of livestock were also received, 13 special livestock trains being run for the inwards traffic and 12 specials for the outwards traffic. Cartage of the exhibits to and from the showground, which was a mile away from the company's Torre station, was effected by the use of six Fordson tractors and six AEC lorries, strengthened by a number of additional Fordson tractors for the cartage of the inwards and outwards livestock. Photographs of the AECs appear earlier in the book.**

Above: How the mighty have fallen! In Chapter 8 you will see this vehicle, a six-wheeled Morris Commercial WD type, working the Devil's Bridge-Plynlimon-Llanidloes service, but it is shown here some years later in use as a tractor fitted with a cab of sorts and a very rough body. It is hauling a converted horse-drawn lorry at the Royal Show, Warwick, on 4 July 1931.

Below: Also at the show, the same converted horse-drawn lorry is being hauled by a Fordson Roadless tractor, Fleet No 2316.

Above: During preparations for the 1931 Royal Show, Fordson tractor No 1194, with special Muir-Hill sprung rear wheels, is hauling a Clayton & Shuttleworth threshing machine to the site. Note that the tractor has double wheels on the front axle.

Below: A portable garage and repair shop was set up specially to deal with any failures during the Royal Show at Warwick. A Fordson tractor is shown under repair – it could be No 2313, judging by the registration number.

Right: Fordson tractor Fleet No 2312 looks very smart, with pneumatic tyres and electric headlamps, at South Lambeth Goods Yard on 16 September 1931.

Centre right: This Fordson tractor has been adapted for shunting by Muir-Hill (Engineering) Ltd – note the coupling hooks. It was photographed on 8 October 1931.

Below: Fleet No 2306, a Rushton tractor built by the Rushton Tractor Co (1929) Ltd, Forest Road, Walthamstow, London, had also been adapted for wagon shunting when it was photographed on 8 October 1931. Note the interesting wagons in the background.

Above: As well as the Swindon scheme, the GWR was also involved in the water pipeline installation for High Wycombe. A Fordson tractor is hauling pipes at Lane End loading bank on 21 January 1932.

Left: A pneumatic-tyred Fordson tractor and solid-rubber-tyred trailer No T.81 await the loading of a 4-ton BX container on 24 April 1929. This trailer was known as the 'Harrow' trailer and was built by the Harrow Industrial Co Ltd, Green Lane Works, Stanley Road, South Harrow, Middlesex.

Left: Pneumatic-tyred Dyson trailer No T.172 is loaded with a 4-ton FX insulated container on 4 November 1932.

Above: The GWR owned a considerable amount of specialised equipment in order that it could carry any type of load offered. This photograph shows 'Warwick' 20-ton solid-tyred trailer No T.169, built by the Eagle Engineering & Motor Co Ltd and photographed near Paddington on 4 November 1932. Note the old type of seat on the front, very much a copy of the horse-drawn variety.

Below and bottom: Six-ton Brockhouse pneumatic-tyred timber trailer No T.319 was built by Brockhouse Ltd of West Bromwich. It is shown here at Bilston in November 1934, after being converted to carry metal strips and/or flat plates.

Above: An Eagle telescopic trailer photographed at South Lambeth Goods Yard on 16 September 1931. Apparently it did not have a number in the GWR fleet, but it is shown as registered with the GWR as it bears 'F. R. E. Davis (Sec) GWR' as was the usual procedure.

Left: No T.252, a 4½-ton timber trailer fitted with solid-rubber-tyred wheels, shows the transition from horse-drawn type to tractor style, or vice versa! It was photographed at Swindon on 11 July 1933.

Below: Eagle 4-ton trailer No T.137 also has solid-rubber-tyred wheels, and was specially designed for conveying containers and for haulage by tractor. Note the interesting road and rail vehicles in the background of this picture taken on 14 November 1934 at Hockley Basin, Birmingham.

Right: Six-ton low-loader trailer No T.109, designed for tractor haulage, was photographed at West Bromwich on 14 November 1934, with a very nice Blake private-owner wagon in the background.

Below: Various company open wagons are in the background of this photograph of Brockhouse 6-ton pneumatic-tyred pole trailer No T.317 at Hockley Basin on 14 November 1934.

Bottom: This 2-ton cattle float trailer, No T.57, with solid tyres, was most probably built by Carrimore. It was also photographed at Hockley Basin on 14 November 1934.

Left: This solid-tyred 5-ton trailer, No T.71, was built by Carrimore Six Wheelers Limited, Great North Road, London N12, and was photographed on 14 November 1934 at Hockley Basin.

Below and bottom: Also photographed on the same occasion were Brockhouse 4-ton container trailer No T.301, complete with pneumatic tyres, and No T.18, a 2-ton Carrimore trailer with fixed sides.

Above: Tasker 4-ton pneumatic-tyred trailer No T.801 was coded Numa D. The seat on the front end, complete with hand-brake, is very reminiscent of horse-drawn practice.

Below: This Scammell 8-ton articulated pole trailer, coded Dyak A, was photographed on 11 July 1944. Note the wartime grey livery.

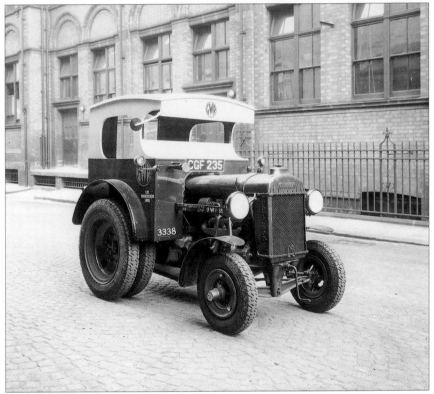

Above: Another Numa D was this 6-ton Carrimore trailer chassis fitted with flat body No T.1196. This trailer was for use behind tractors; note once again the seat at the front reminiscent of horse-drawn vehicles. It was photographed at Swindon on 12 May 1936.

Centre left and left: This immaculate Fordson tractor, No 3338, is just out of the works, fitted with Firestone pneumatic tyres, and electric tail, side and headlamps. Note that the speed with a pneumatic-tyred trailer was 20mph, but with solid tyres it was only 12mph. The photograph was taken on 21 October 1935.

175

Above and below: In early 1939 the GWR purchased a Latil tractor fitted with producer gas apparatus. Producer gas was generated from coal in a gas-making plant carried on the vehicle. Under certain conditions it was more economical in working than either petrol or oil. It was also in the national interest, with war looming, to use an alternative to imported fuel. This vehicle (Latil Tractor No S419 [Cie des Automobiles Industrielles Latil]) was used on cartage work in the Cardiff area. A standard petrol engine was modified to work on the fuel produced. The essentials of the apparatus were a small furnace, together with a storage tank and a cleansing device. The coal was supplied by Powell Duffryn Associated Collieries at Ystrad Mynach.

Chapter 8:
Motor Omnibuses

It is well known that because the Great Western Railway thought that £85,000 was a large sum to spend on the construction of a light railway between Helston and The Lizard, a decision was made to run a 'Road Motor' service between the two points. The service started on 17 August 1903 and made history as the first GWR bus service. The two vehicles used were purchased from Sir George Newnes, who in May 1903 had introduced a feeder service between Ilfracombe and Blackmoor on the Lynton & Barnstaple Railway; however, owing to police objections to speeds in excess of 8mph, he was persuaded to sell the vehicles to the GWR. These two Milnes-Daimlers were of the wagonette type, but were rebuilt later with enclosed bodies. Three daily return trips were run between Helston and The Lizard, with intermediate stops at Ruan Major, Penhale, Cury Cross Lanes and Lemarth. The single fare was 1s 6d (7½p).

An official report, dated 2 September 1903, stated that '...on the previous week 668 passengers and some 20 parcels were conveyed. Receipts were £45 (an average of 17s 10d [89p] per trip). On fine days there were more passengers than could be conveyed. A 3rd car is required. Since inauguration of service absolute punctuality has been maintained.'

When one considers what the road surfaces were like, full of ruts, extremely muddy in winter and very dusty in summer, the vehicles stood up very well. Indeed, owing to the very bad road conditions the service was suspended from October 1904 to April 1905 as the GWR considered an omnibus too expensive a vehicle to be used as a steam-roller! Helston Rural District Council refused to roll the road, and as there were apparently no steam-rollers in Cornwall to do the job, the GWR sent one of its own to Cornwall County Council to get the road back to a reasonable state. A fire at Helston Garage, which destroyed two vehicles, also delayed the resumption of services.

Incidentally, the Helston-Lizard service, together with others instigated up to late in 1904, were run contrary to legal requirements. While the Locomotives on Highways Act of 1896 had done away with the man carrying a red flag, it applied only to vehicles under 3 tons in weight. As manufacturers could not produce omnibuses to comply with this requirement, advantage was taken of the fact that no regulations were in existence stating what should be included in the weight of the vehicle; certain items were therefore removed, and the chassis painted as '2 tons 19 cwts'. The regulations were modified in 1904 to allow the use of

Below: **A cartoon of the Lampeter-Aberayron 'Road Motor' as depicted by a local artist, which appeared in the** *Great Western Railway Magazine* **in 1907.**

vehicles up to 5 tons in weight without a pilot. Also, as regulations under the Motor Car Act of 1903 had not been formulated, the first three GWR vehicles had no registration plates.

During the first few years the Great Western Railway held a very prominent position as the pioneer of motor services. Other railway companies also purchased road motors but never pursued their services quite so vigorously as the GWR.

The policy in the beginning was to run the omnibuses strictly as feeders, it being considered not prudent to run between places connected by rail, however circuitous the railway route might be. This resulted in people refraining from travelling except in cases of real necessity, and later experience proved that a direct service created traffic. All early services were separate establishments, which greatly increased the operating costs.

At the end of 1904 the Great Western Railway employed more omnibuses than London, so its working experiences attracted attention and brought enquiries from all over the world. From a small start in 1903, with two Milnes-Daimler passenger vehicles, the company had 34 by the end of 1904, 95 in 1907, and in 1927 the total had risen to 300.

By about 1905 so many operators required motor omnibuses that it became increasingly difficult to acquire them, London's omnibus services absorbing nearly all that could be produced. The ideal requirement for the GWR was the Milnes-Daimler type, which was regarded as the company's standard. However, only a few were readily available and the company had to be satisfied with Wolseley, Durkopp and Clarkson steam cars, all of which gave trouble. In fact, it was seriously considered in 1906 that the GWR should design and build its own omnibuses.

The fleet remained fairly steady without substantial increase until the start of World War 1 in 1914. During the war some services were relinquished to other companies who were prepared to run them, and in 1919 the GWR came under Parliamentary obligation to withdraw its Wolverhampton and Bridgnorth service as Wolverhampton Corporation desired to operate it. However, that body was not ready to take over the service until 1923, by which time it was firmly established and was a considerable loss to the Great Western when it passed out of its hands in that year.

Serious competition grew steadily after World War 1 when many small companies and independent owners came into existence, in

Below: Milnes-Daimler wagonette No 1 at The Lizard on 15 August 1903. The engine was a four-cylinder Cannstatt-Daimler governed by a throttle and giving 16bhp at 800rpm, with Sims Bosch magneto ignition. The drive was through a cone-clutch gearcase and a universally jointed propeller shaft to the differential and cross-shaft. The gearbox was arranged to give four speeds and reverse from 3 to 14mph. The road wheels were driven from the cross-shaft by pinion, with large gears being fixed to the wheels; however, this arrangement was very noisy and upset the Metropolitan Police when similar vehicles were tried in London. Three brakes were fitted, one working on the record speed shaft (drive shaft) and the other two on drums fitted to the driving pinions. There was also a screw-type brake for emergencies and for holding the car when it had to be stopped on a hill. Solid rubber tyres were used on all wheels, those on the rear driving wheels being 6 inches wide. The body was of the open wagonette type with a light roof, having 20 seats inside plus room for two on the driver's seat. Petrol from the rear tank was forced by the engine exhaust gas to supply the single-jet carburettor. Plain bearings were fitted throughout and there were wick-fed lubricators. The solid rubber tyres cost about £200 per set, and it was common for one or more to leave the wheel in the first few hundred miles. However, petrol was cheap at fourpence per gallon.

Above: Timetable of the GWR's Helston-Lizard service from 18 July 1904.

Top right: Milnes-Daimler wagonette No 1 leaving Helston for The Lizard on a preliminary run on 15 August 1903, prior to the service starting on the 17th. Trouble was experienced with the gearbox on this trip owing to the fact that a part was missing – it hadn't been put in by the manufacturer!

Centre right: Milnes-Daimler wagonettes Nos 1 (right) and 2 at The Lizard on 15 August 1903.

Right: No 1 leaving Helston on 17 August 1903, the first day of the service to The Lizard.

turn being absorbed by large concerns, proving all very harassing to the GWR. In 1925 the company's rights to develop its omnibus services were questioned by the London & Provincial Omnibus Owners Association in respect of services in the West of England and North Wales, and as a result agreements were entered into with the Devon & Cornwall Motor Transport and Crosville companies.

The Western National Omnibus Company was formed in January 1929, and this combined the road services of the GWR and the National Omnibus & Transport Company in Devon and Cornwall. Later the railway linked its interests with the British Electric Traction Co Ltd. Further absorptions of road interests took place in

other areas of the Great Western system, involving such concerns as Western Welsh, Crosville, Thames Valley Traction, Midland Red, City of Oxford and Bristol Tramways. On the last day of 1933 the final omnibus in GWR brown and cream livery was handed over to the associated Southern National Omnibus Company at Weymouth. Thus ended, after almost 30 years, the history of the independent Great Western Railway road passenger services.

For further information on GWR motor omnibuses see *Railway Motor Buses and Bus Services in the British Isles 1902-1933, Volume II*, by John Cummings (OPC).

Right: From 17 August to 17 October 1903 both the open cars were run, but from 19 October one luggage motor omnibus seating 18 passengers and carrying luggage and parcels was substituted for the winter traffic. This photograph shows No 1 as converted to an enclosed vehicle. The livery appears to be just varnished timber.

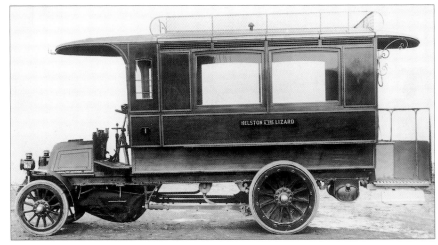

Right: The motor omnibus service between Marazion, Penzance and Newlyn started on 31 October 1903. This picture shows the first double-deck omnibus to be run by the GWR, 20hp Milnes-Daimler No 6, at Penzance in 1904.

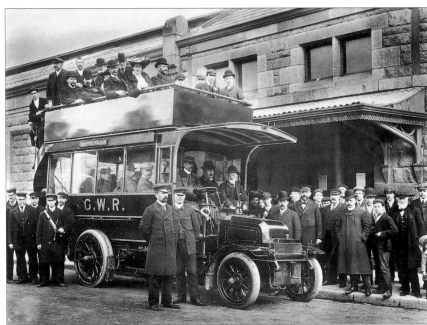

Below: No 5, a 20hp Milnes-Daimler, is working the first trip of the Slough-Farnham Common-Beaconsfield service on 1 March 1904. The photograph clearly shows the varnished wood livery.

Above: This is No 5 again, on the Slough-Stoke Poges-Burnham Beeches service in 1904.
The body was built by Thrupp & Maberley of London.

Below: Another view of No 5 at the Royal Hotel on the same service in 1904.

Right: On 22 August 1904 Milnes-Daimler double-deck omnibus No 16 is seen on the Torquay and Paignton service, which had started on 11 July. The driver appears to be sitting well back to keep out of the waves! Most of the omnibus bodies at this time were built by Messrs Dodson.

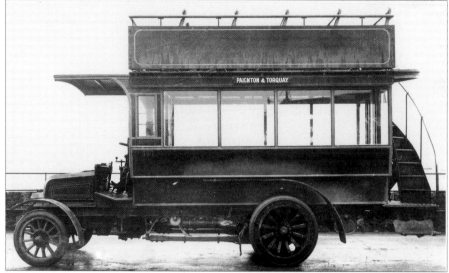

Right: Milnes-Daimler 20hp 'Jersey' car No 19 is seen at Slough in 1904. These vehicles were used mostly on private outings, and, as can be seen, a ladder was required to reach most of the seats.

Below: Milnes-Daimler 20hp double-deck omnibus No 7 at Slough station in 1904. Judging by the advertisements it was presumably on the Slough-Windsor service, which started on 18 July 1904 to supplement rail services. Notice the board bearing the driver's name, C. L. Hayward, just under the vehicle number. The GWR livery is much more apparent here.

Left: Milnes-Daimler 20hp single-deck omnibus No 12 with roof luggage compartment at Slough in April 1904.

Left: Milnes-Daimler 20hp double-deck omnibus No 17 is at Slough in April 1904 on the Slough, Eton & Windsor service. Note the brake shoes acting on the exterior of the rear wheels.

Below: Milnes-Daimler 16hp motor wagonette No 20, with a roof luggage rack, was photographed at Swindon Works in 1904 after emerging from the paint shop in superb Great Western livery. The picture is so sharp that it is possible to read the manufacturer's name on the tyres – Peters Union Frankfurt AM.

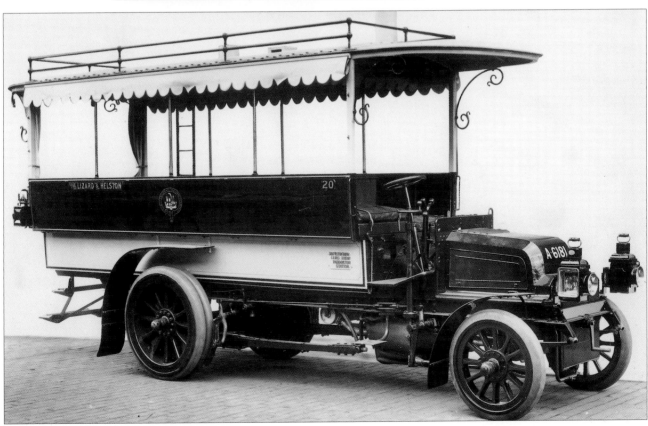

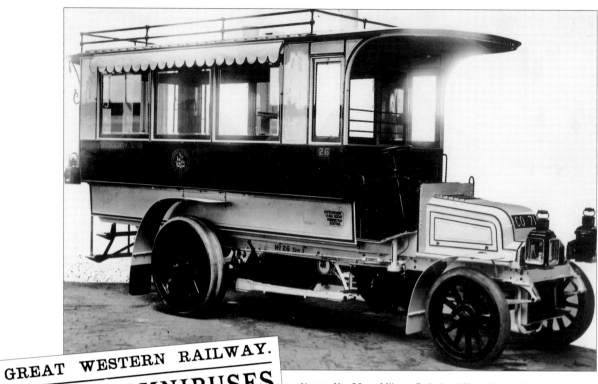

GREAT WESTERN RAILWAY.

MOTOR OMNIBUSES

BETWEEN

SLOUGH and WINDSOR

STATIONS
(VIA ETON.)

Commencing on Monday July 18th, Motor Omnibuses will run between the above points as under :

SLOUGH TO WINDSOR.—Week Days.

	a.m.	a.m.	a.m.	noon	p.m.	p.m.	p.m.	p.m.	p.m.	p.m.	p.m.	p.m.	p.m.	p.m.
Slough Station - dep.	9. 0	10. 0	11. 0	12. 0	1. 0	2. 0	3. 0	4. 0	5. 0	6. 0	7. 0	8. 0	9. 0	
Windsor (G.W.) Station - arr.abt.	9.15	10.15	11.15	12.15	1.15	2.15	3.15	4.15	5.15	6.15	7.15	8.15	9.15	

WINDSOR TO SLOUGH.—Week Days.

	a.m.	a.m.	a.m.	noon	p.m.	p.m.	p.m.	p.m.	p.m.	p.m.	p.m.	p.m.	p.m.
Windsor (G.W.) Station - dep.	9.30	10.30	11.30	12.30	1.30	2.30	3.30	4.30	5.30	6.30	7.30	8.30	9.30
Slough Station arr.abt.	9.45	10.45	11.45	12.45	1.45	2.45	3.45	4.45	5.45	6.45	7.45	8.45	9.45

The Motor Omnibuses will run via High Street, Slough, and call at Eton and other points as required in each direction.

FARES :

| Between Slough and Windsor | - | - | - | - | 3d. |
| Between Slough and Eton or Windsor and Eton | - | - | - | 2d. |

Single Tickets only will be issued on the Motor Omnibuses and must be retained until completion of the journey.

Books of 24 Tickets, available by the Company's Omnibuses between Slough and Windsor, can be obtained at the Booking Offices at Slough and Windsor at a charge of 5s. 6d.

FULL FARES TO BE PAID FOR ALL SEATS OCCUPIED.

TIME TABLES.—The Directors give notice that the Company do not undertake that the Motor Omnibuses shall start or arrive at the time specified in the Bills ; nor will they be accountable for any loss, inconvenience, or injury, which may arise from delay or detention.

THROUGH RAILWAY TICKETS WILL NOT BE ISSUED ON, NOR BY THESE MOTOR CARS.

For any further information respecting the arrangements shewn in this handbill, application should be made to Mr. W. A. Hart, Divisional Superintendent, Paddington Station.

JAMES C. INGLIS, General Manager.

PADDINGTON, July, 1904.

WYMAN & SONS, Ltd., Printers, Fetter Lane, London, E.C., and Reading.—19543s.

L.D
(15,000)

Above: No 26, a Milnes-Daimler 16hp single-deck luggage omnibus, was photographed at Swindon Works in May 1904, and is carrying a destination board for Albaston, Callington and Saltash. This service replaced a private horse bus that started on 1 June 1904, and to which the GWR had paid a subsidy of £156. This was one of the vehicles that had a white bonnet.

Left: Timetable for the Slough-Windsor service.

Right: The interior of No 26 shows that the similarity between it and London Underground stock is quite marked, particularly the straps for standing passengers. The photograph was taken in 1904 at Swindon. Also note the droplight with a leather strap.

Above: A line-up of Milnes-Daimler 'road motors' at Slough station in 1904. From left to right, they are a luggage omnibus, a 'Jersey' car, three single-deck omnibuses, and a double-decker.

Above: Another view of Slough station in 1904, with a selection of 20hp Milnes-Daimler vehicles. From left to right they are 'Jersey' car No 19, single-deck No 20 on the Windsor service, single-deck Nos 13 and 5 on the Beaconsfield service, and a double-decker on the Windsor service.

Above: More vehicles photographed at Slough station in 1905. On the left is a 24hp Straker Squire double-decker (one-man operation), then second and fourth are 30hp Milnes-Daimler double-deck omnibuses, and third and fifth are 30hp Milnes-Daimler single-deckers. On the right is a Clarkson 20hp steam car.

Right: Timetable and fares for the Slough-Beaconsfield service in 1904.

Below: Milnes-Daimler 20hp single-deck omnibus No 5, fitted with four oil headlamps, near Beaconsfield, probably on the first trip of this service, which started on 1 March 1904. The diabolical road surface can be seen.

Left: A 20hp Clarkson steam omnibus is shown here in one of the squares near Paddington prior to going into service. This vehicle was used with two others on the Wolverhampton-Bridgnorth service, which started on 7 November 1904. These steam omnibuses gave considerable boiler trouble and were replaced by Milnes-Daimlers, but prior to being sold they saw further service in Somerset.

Above: Clarkson steam omnibus No 36 is seen at Bridgnorth in 1904. The fare between Bridgnorth and Wolverhampton was 11d.

Right: Milnes-Daimler 20hp composite single-deck omnibus No 8 is seen at Helston station in 1904 – note the acetylene lamp on the front of the roof. This vehicle was placed on the service on 31 March 1904 for goods, mail and passengers (ten inside and two beside the driver). The goods compartment could also be used by passengers by means of flap seats, and smoking was allowed in this compartment.

Above: No 8 poses for the photographer on Bochym Hill near Mullion, between The Lizard and Helston, in 1904.

Right: From 1 May 1904 the General Post Office entered into a contract with the Great Western 'Road Motors' to carry mails between Helston and The Lizard. This photograph, taken about 1912, shows one of the 20hp Dennis single-deck omnibuses at Ruan Crossroads exchanging mails with the local postman and his donkey cart.

Below: Another view of the Dennis, this time exchanging passengers at Ruan Crossroads. It appears to be a general interchange between the GWR 'Road Motor' and the local stagecoach.

Above: The Calne-Marlborough route in Wiltshire started on 10 October 1904, and this 20hp Milnes-Daimler double-deck omnibus is shown outside the Red Lion at Avebury in 1907. Apart from a few minor alterations this particular location has changed very little.

Left: Milnes-Daimler 20hp double-deck omnibus No 31 was also photographed at Avebury outside the well-known hostelry, in about 1909.

Left: A third view at Avebury, with 20hp Dennis single-deck omnibus No 158 outside the same public house about 1911.

Above: Another view of 20hp Milnes-Daimler No 5, this time at Marlborough on the service from Calne circa 1908. The livery is now brown and cream.

Below: No 92, a 30hp Milnes-Daimler charabanc on the Aberayron to Aberystwyth service, is shown here on the summer-only extension to New Quay. The photograph was taken in 1907.

Left: Maudslay 14hp 14-seat single-deck omnibus No 52 was photographed at Slough in 1905. It was one of three vehicles ordered from that manufacturer, and was used on the Slough-Langley-Colnbrook service, which started on 8 May 1905.

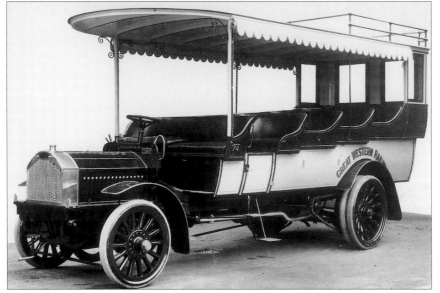

Left: This is Durkopp 20hp observation car, or covered charabanc, No 74. Its chassis was built by Durkoppwerke AG, Reinickendorf, Bielefeld, Germany, and was photographed on 24 August 1905 at Swindon Works, where the body was built to the design of Mr F. C. A. Coventry, Motor Car Assistant to the Superintendent of the Line. The vehicle accommodated 30 passengers and was closed at the back by glass panels that obviated any inconvenience from dust. A cast plate on the front screen stated that the chassis was supplied by the Motor Car Emporium Ltd, London W, which was also stamped on the front wheel bosses. These Durkopp vehicles were ordered because of the previously mentioned shortage of Milnes-Daimlers, but were constantly in trouble with broken crankshafts; because of the difficulty of obtaining spares, they were cannibalised to keep the remainder working.

Right: This Straker Squire 24hp chassis has been fitted with an experimental front-entrance double-deck body built by G. Scammell & Nephew Ltd, Fashion Street, Spitalfields, London E1. This vehicle was used in the Slough area, but did not prove successful and was later fitted with a more conventional staircase. It was also said that there were complaints from female passengers using the staircase that they did not like the drivers looking at their ankles! This photograph is dated 27 September 1905.

Above: Both horse-drawn and motor vehicle bodies are shown in the Road Motor Shop at Swindon Works on 25 July 1907. It is noticeable that the numberplates are missing; therefore one may assume rightly or wrongly that, like steam locomotives, the body and chassis need not have remained together all their life.

Below: No 117, a 30hp Milnes-Daimler single-deck omnibus, is new out of the shops on what appears to be a trial run circa 1910. This vehicle is virtually a charabanc-type body, but fitted with windows and roof.

Above: As with everything else, the GWR was very conscious of the impact of advertising, and hit on the idea of sending 'road motors' to various parts of the country to publicise places of interest on the system. These two pictures show 30hp Wolseley double-deck omnibus No 63 prior to setting off on one of these tours about 1908. On a similar tour a 'road motor' left Slough for Scotland on 4 November 1907, reaching Carlisle on the 7th. From there its route was via Dumfries, Ayr, Paisley, Glasgow, Crieff, Inverness, Elgin, Banff, Aberdeen, Dundee, St Andrews, Stirling and Edinburgh. After this 2,479-mile tour it returned to Slough early in 1908.

Below: It is almost certain that this poster was issued in 1907 to publicise the Llandyssil-New Quay service, which started on 1 May 1907, and it is therefore one of the earliest double royal posters produced by the Great Western Railway to advertise its road motor omnibus services. The vehicle depicted is artistically represented as a 30hp Milnes-Daimler.

Above: The GWR had a great aptitude for using corrugated iron; one only had to look at its stations and halts to see the curious 'pagoda' huts that graced the platforms. Another adaptation is shown here. The *Great Western Railway Magazine* stated in its issue of October 1908: 'The above photograph shows a new type of standard motor car shed which has been adapted. It comprises a car shed, stores hut, small workshop, office and is a considerable improvement on the former system of separate huts.' There was not much clearance in the width or height, and the top flaps were opened only for double-deckers. This 20hp Milnes-Daimler is shown at Stroud.

Right: The omnibus service between Carmarthen and Llanstephan started on 1 May 1909, and this photograph was probably taken just after that date on a glorious summer's day at The Square, Llanstephan. The driver appears to be standing under the lamp on the left, and his vehicle is a 30hp single-deck Milnes-Daimler.

Left: Milnes-Daimler 30hp single-deck omnibus No 41 is fresh out of Swindon paint shop (paint date 6 April 1910, and photographed on the 11th) ready to go on the road for another advertising tour. The vehicle is fitted with shaft drive and the exterior brake acting on the tyres of the wheels has also been dispensed with.

Right: The body of Dennis 20hp single-deck omnibus No 156 was built by Swindon Works (paint date 23 May 1910), and, as can be seen, the coachwork is very railway-like in its appearance.

Bottom left: Bell End Motor Halt was on the Stourbridge-Bromsgrove route, a service that started on 13 February 1905 between Stourbridge and Belbroughton, being extended to Bromsgrove in 1910. This picture gives an idea of what must have been a very typical scene on many of the Great Western omnibus routes.

Below: A GWR Motor Car Department dimensional drawing of the Dennis 30cwt chassis, intended for body builders.

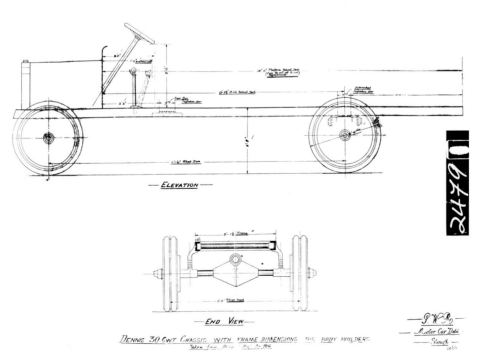

— ELEVATION —

— END VIEW —

DENNIS 30 CWT CHASSIS WITH FRAME DIMENSIONS FOR BODY BUILDERS

Scale: 7mm/ft.

195

Above: This 'swarm' of GWR omnibuses was photographed on excursion workings to Ascot, circa 1912.

Below: The small 16-20hp Straker Squire omnibuses were purchased in 1910 and fitted with 'observation' bodies for use on excursion trips. This vehicle was photographed at Swindon and bears a paint date of 4 October 1911.

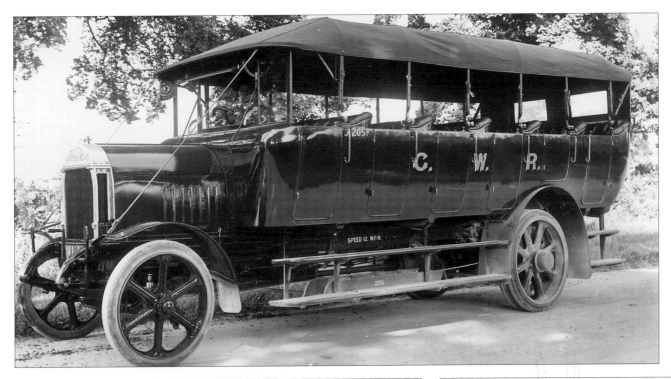

Top: Fifteen of these Maudslay 35hp chassis were ordered in 1913 and were very successful, being fitted with various types of body. Charabanc No 205 was photographed on 28 June 1914; a ladder, also numbered 205, was provided for easy access.

Above: No 213 was another 35hp Maudslay chassis, photographed at Slough with a double-deck body and gas bag. During World War 1 the GWR adapted many vehicles to run on coal gas because of the shortage of petrol. The biggest difficulty, apparently, was keeping the gas bag anchored to the top of the bus – in very windy weather some drivers had to chase their gas bags over fields. About 250 cubic feet of coal gas provided power equivalent to 1 gallon of petrol. It is understood that the firm of H. D. Bowyer is still extant.

Left: A delightful rear view of the coal gas converted vehicle No 213. One wonders if the Zilvo advert was displayed only on gas bag vehicles...

Right and centre right: No 232, an AEC 3½-ton chassis with an enclosed single-deck body, was photographed on 21 August 1923. As already described, these ex-Army chassis were fitted with transferable coach or cartage bodies. This particular vehicle became a lorry in 1928.

Below: Another view of No 232 taken at Swindon Works on 11 January 1923, where the large saloon body was designed and built. The ventilation was carefully considered, and hinged droplights in front and ventilators to the rear of the passenger compartment ensured a good current of air. The seats were made of light open metal supports instead of the wooden variety formerly used. Gangway hinged seats were installed, which could be swung neatly under the main seats when not required, and electric lighting was fitted. There were trap doors in the floor to give easy access to parts of the chassis. Twenty-two vehicles with this type of body were built.

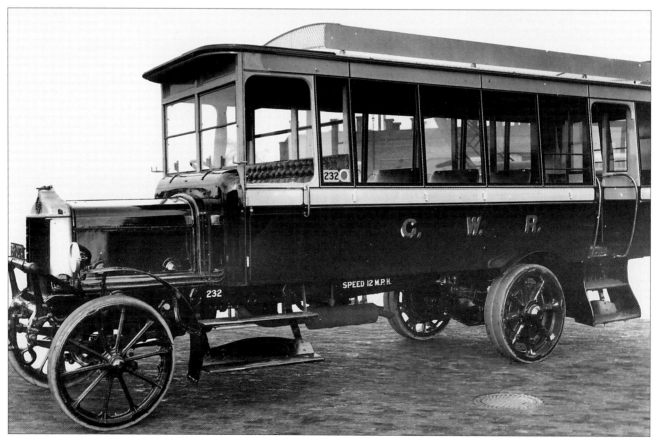

Above: Further views of the front and rear of omnibus No 232 at Slough on 28 November 1922, showing various differences.

Below: This AEC 3½-ton chassis was photographed with a charabanc body at Swindon in May 1924. Compare this picture with that on page 94, where the vehicle is shown as a lorry.

This page: Because the AEC 3½-ton vehicles were rather large for some of the narrow roads traversed on some routes, there was a requirement for a lighter vehicle, and an order was placed for 10 Chevrolets. The first photograph shows one of these 22hp 14-seat single-deck omnibuses, supplied by the Chevrolet Motor Co, Detroit, Michigan, USA, at Slough on 30 August 1924. Note the pneumatic tyres. The other two photographs, taken on the same day, show a sister omnibus fitted with an open body and collapsible hood.

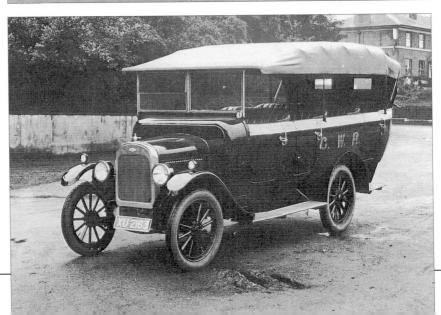

Above: In the Annual Report for 1926 from the Superintendent of Road Transport, presented to the Traffic Committee meeting on 28 April 1927, it was stated that a shelter at Mathry Cross, on the Fishguard-St David's route, had been supplied by Messrs Pratten & Co of Midsomer Norton at a cost of £22 10s 0d including erection. These shelters lasted for many years.

Below: No 565 is a Burford forward-control 30cwt chassis fitted with an 18-seater single-deck saloon body by Messrs Bartle, and is shown here on the Mathry station to St David's service, which started on 1 August 1923. The photograph was taken at about that time.

Above and below: No 806, a 23hp Burford forward-control chassis, has a Buckingham charabanc body. The front view, with the doors open, is a bit reminiscent of the broad gauge! The photograph was taken at Kingsbridge in September 1924, and the vehicle became a lorry in 1929.

Above and left: No 813, a 23hp Burford forward-control chassis with a Swindon-built full-front body, is operating the Farnham Common service at Slough on 12 March 1925. Between them, H. G. Burford & Co Ltd and the GWR did much to develop the forward-control system in order to give more room for the body on the chassis. This vehicle carried both electric and oil lamps. Note the Hackney carriage plate on the rear.

Left: No 859, another full-fronted body on a 23hp Burford forward-control chassis, was photographed at Swindon on 10 May 1925. This vehicle became a lorry in 1928.

Above and below: No 228, an AEC 3½-ton saloon omnibus, stands at Kingsbridge on 17 March 1925. In this instance the vehicle has acetylene headlamps, and was rebuilt as a lorry the following year.

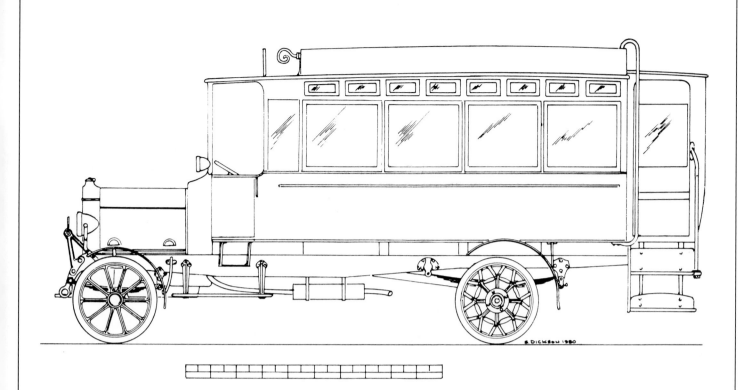

This drawing was prepared from basic dimensions taken from a weight diagram, other details were estimated from photographs. It is shown with a representative body and with electric lighting.

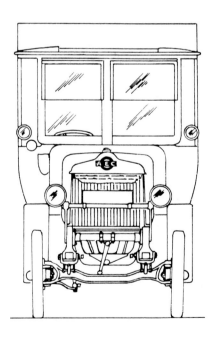
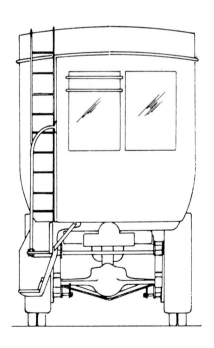

Above: Scale drawing of the 3¹/₂-ton AEC omnibus. The drawing has been prepared from basic dimensions taken from a weight diagram, and the other details have been estimated from the accompanying photographs. It is shown with a representative body and electric lighting.

This page: **The three photographs of No 914, a Thornycroft 30cwt 25hp A1 chassis fitted with a front-entrance Swindon-built saloon omnibus body, were taken at Slough, the side views in October 1925 and the rear view on 30 January 1926. Later in the book this omnibus is shown with a modified body at Swindon prior to an advertising trip on 7 April 1930.**

Above: No 1202, a 30hp Maudslay ML 3 chassis with a John Buckingham 32-seat single-deck saloon body, stands at Slough in 1927. This vehicle incorporated all the improvements of that time, such as pneumatic tyres, four-wheel brakes and ground gears. It was sold to the Thames Valley Traction Company in 1931.

Above: No 1280 is a Guy FBB chassis with a John Buckingham 'all weather'-type body, and is seen at Torquay in June 1927. These vehicles were increasingly used for land cruises such as to Dartmoor, North Wales, etc. No 1280 was eventually sold to the Western National Omnibus Company in 1929.

Above: No 1278, another Guy FBB chassis, has a Vickers of Dartford saloon body, and was also photographed at Torquay in May 1927. It was sold to Western Transport, later Crosville, in 1929.

Right: Another view of No 1278, at Slough in May 1927.

Below: Side and rear elevation of a Guy FBB chassis, has a Vickers of Dartford saloon body.

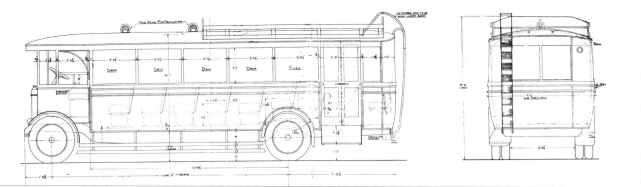

Scale: 4mm/ft

Centre right: Another chassis fitted with a saloon body by Vickers of Dartford was Maudslay 30hp ML3 No 1552, shown here at Slough in 1928. This vehicle was sold to Western National in 1929.

Below: This is Maudslay ML3 No 1550 with the same body as the vehicle in the previous picture after a tree fell on it at Farnham Common! Earlier in the book the same vehicle is depicted as a cattle lorry after a rebuild.

Above and below: These splendid pictures of No 1202, a Maudslay ML3 30hp chassis fitted with a 32-seat John Buckingham body, were taken at Slough in September 1926. The vehicle was sold to Thames Valley Traction Co Ltd in 1931.

Above: At Stroud on 1 November 1927 is a Maudslay ML3 chassis with a John Buckingham 'all weather' body. Note that the driver's cab has a solid roof and that the bonnet is polished aluminium. Contrast this with the painted bonnets on similar vehicles on page 208. These vehicles were used for land cruises or excursions, and No 1222 was sold to Western National in 1929.

Centre right and right: Another John Buckingham 'all weather' body has been fitted to No 1229, a Maudslay ML3B, seen at Bristol Temple Meads on 11 May 1928. The first picture shows the hood closed, while the second shows it open. This vehicle is shown as designated for a land cruise, but presumably not without its registration plates, which were YW 1721. It was eventually sold to the Thames Valley Traction Co in 1931. It is interesting to note that the station clock shows 12 noon in the first picture and 12.25 in the second – did it take all that time to open the omnibus roof?

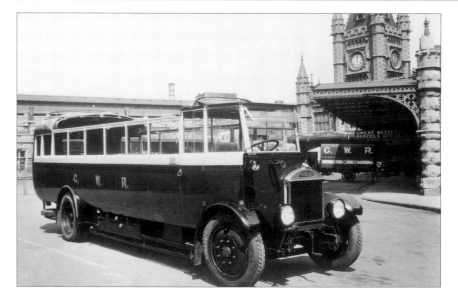

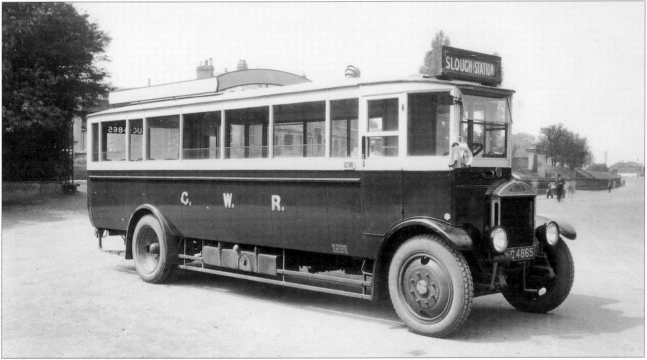

Top and above: **No 1238 is a Maudslay ML3 chassis with a John Buckingham saloon body, and is seen at Slough on 14 May 1928.** Note the blind indicator box fitted above the roof, the railway-type roof ventilator, and the polished metal bonnet cover. No 1238 was sold to the Thames Valley Traction Co in 1931.

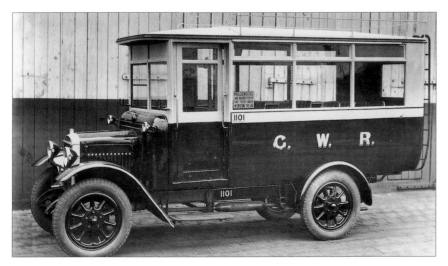

Left: No 1101, a delightful lightweight Morris Commercial saloon omnibus, poses at Swindon Works on 9 September 1928. Its Swindon-built front-entrance body was later rebuilt into a commercial vehicle, and it has the same chassis as vehicle No 1122 (page 88).

Top: No 1658 is a Guy OND 2-ton 25-seater saloon omnibus with a GWR front-entrance body, photographed at Swindon Works on 3 September 1929. It was eventually sold to the Bristol Tramways & Carriage Company.

Above and right: The exterior and interior of No 1298, a Thornycroft A6 chassis with an 'all weather' body, were photographed at Swindon on 8 January 1930. This vehicle had a six-cylinder engine and a maximum permitted speed of 20mph. It was fully fitted with both interior and exterior electric light, and one can see that the seating arrangement was very confined and the layout staggered.

Above: No 883, a Burford ND forward-control chassis fitted with a charabanc body, is seen at Corris in July 1928 en route to Machynlleth. This vehicle became a lorry in March 1929.

Below: A meeting of Maudslays at Bovey Tracey, ready to depart, after loading, for excursions to Dartmoor. All these ML3s, Fleet Nos 1224, 1229, 1524, 1529 and two unidentified, were sold in 1929.

This spread: No 1601, a sumptuous vehicle built for the Oxford to Cheltenham service, was photographed at Slough on 14 March 1929 prior to its introduction. It had a Gilford OT forward-control chassis with a six-cylinder engine, and the 22-seat body was built by Wycombe Motor Bodies Ltd.

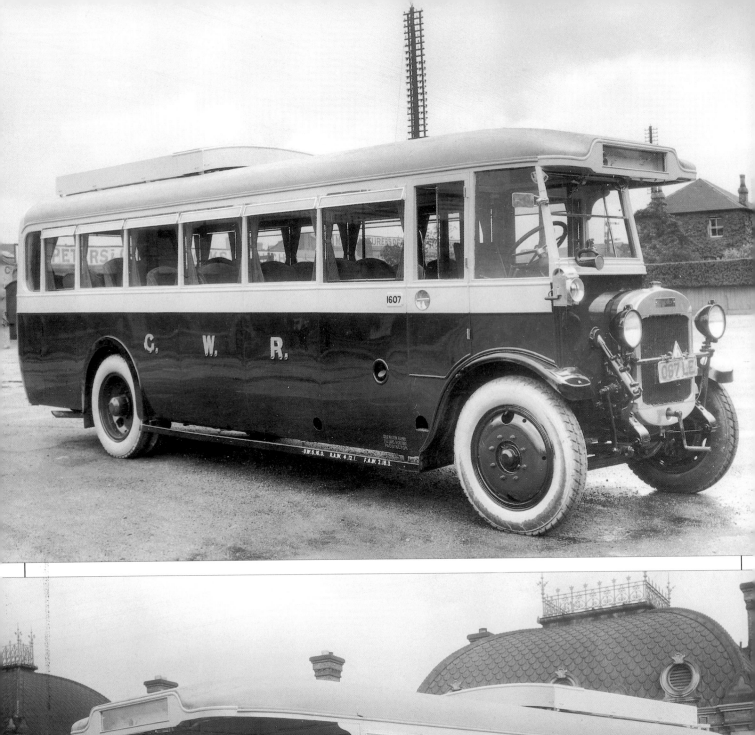

This spread: No 1607, a Thornycroft FY, BC forward-control chassis with a 26-seat single-deck body by Vickers of Dartford, was also used on the Oxford-Cheltenham service. This very nice vehicle was photographed inside and out at Slough on 2 August 1929.

Above and below: Two 30cwt Thornycroft 25hp A1 chassis fitted with Swindon-built omnibus bodies stand at Swindon station on 7 April 1930 prior to an advertising tour. Both vehicles became lorries shortly after the tour was over.

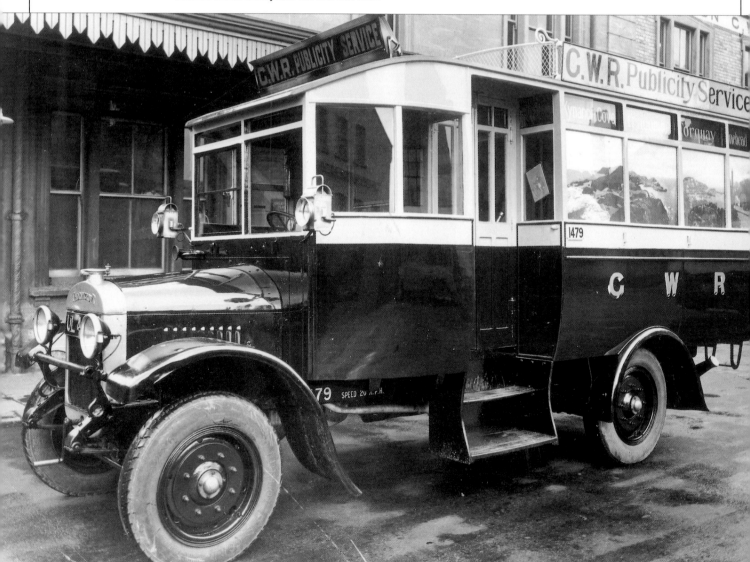

G.W.R.– Thornycroft A1 Omnibus

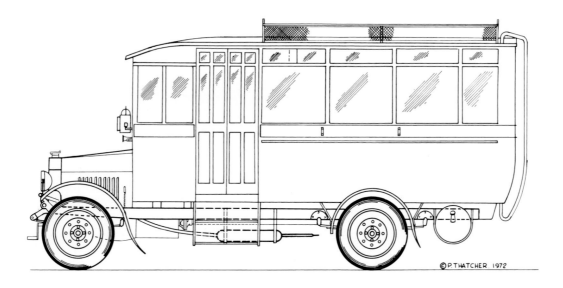

© P.THATCHER. 1972

Scale 7mm/1ft

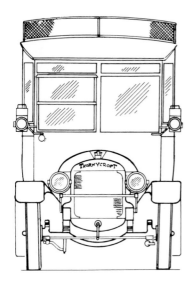

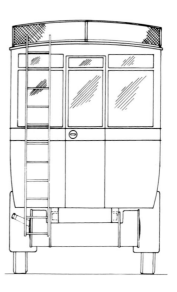

FEET

Above: **Scale drawing of a Thornycroft A1 omnibus.**

Right: No 1468, a Thornycroft A1 chassis with a single-deck omnibus body, is seen here at Highclere on 5 August 1932. This vehicle was shown in the records as being sold to London General Country Services on 15 November 1931. One wonders where the vehicle is destined, as it is running under trade plates and is still in GWR livery.

Below: Guy OND 25-seater saloon No 1651 is on the Paddington-Victoria inter-station service in September 1930. This service was undertaken by two vehicles (Nos 1650 and 1651) carrying passengers booked through from the GWR and the Continent and vice versa, and was later taken over by London Transport. Both 1650 and 1651 became lorries in 1933; the latter can be seen on page 100.

Right: This six-wheeled Morris Commercial WD vehicle was used for the Aberystwyth, Devil's Bridge, Plynlimon and Llanidloes service. The service from Devil's Bridge via Plynlimon to Llanidloes commenced in July 1925. According to the *Great Western Railway Magazine*, it started from Aberystwyth in the mornings from 2 August 1928, and in the afternoons passengers travelled by the Vale of Rheidol Railway to Devil's Bridge, where they joined the bus. The vehicle was a type used by the Army and had an eight-speed gearbox, so was suited to running over rough country. The body was uncovered because a hood was not much use in the very high winds. Each of the 12 passengers carried was provided with an apron for protection against the mountain mist encountered on the high slopes. This was the first excursion of its kind in Britain, and the vehicle was entirely controlled by the engine – the brakes were used only in emergencies.

Chapter 9:
Miscellaneous Vehicles

Above and below: In June 1926, to meet the need for a cheaper unit for small collections and deliveries, the GWR introduced a number of 'Carette' motor tricycle carriers on an experimental basis. These vehicles enabled the company to provide a special service for urgent perishable consignments, the idea being to economise on transport by not using expensive equipment on all cartage. It is interesting that the GWR also used ordinary pedal tricycles on some duties.

Above: This is one of the three motor tricycle 'auto carriers' that the Great Western Railway introduced into London in 1910. One was used for express parcel delivery from Paddington, another for conveying advertising literature in the heart of London, and the third on parcel deliveries in the Acton area.

Above and below: Burford 15cwt petrol trolley No 346 was used on the harbour at St Helier, Jersey, Channel Islands, another GWR outpost.

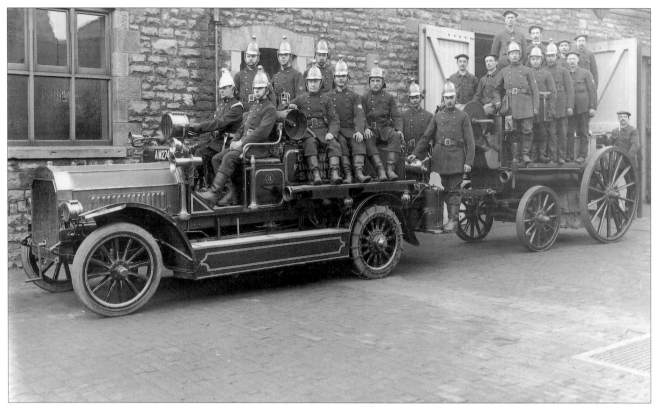

Above: Fire precautions were always, and still are, a very high priority on railway premises. This photograph shows part of the Swindon Works Fire Brigade in 1916. The leading vehicle is a petrol-engined fire engine built by Dennis Bros of Guildford, towing a four-wheeled oil-fired steam fire engine. Everything looks in tiptop condition, and they were even prepared for extremely bad weather judging by the chains on the back wheels.

Below: This very dilapidated Morris Commercial van was dragged off the scrap-heap to convey fire-fighting equipment and haul a World War 2 fire trailer pump. On board, in July 1940, are trained firemen, members of the GWR staff. The dustbin contained sand for use on incendiary bombs.

Scale: 10mm/ft.

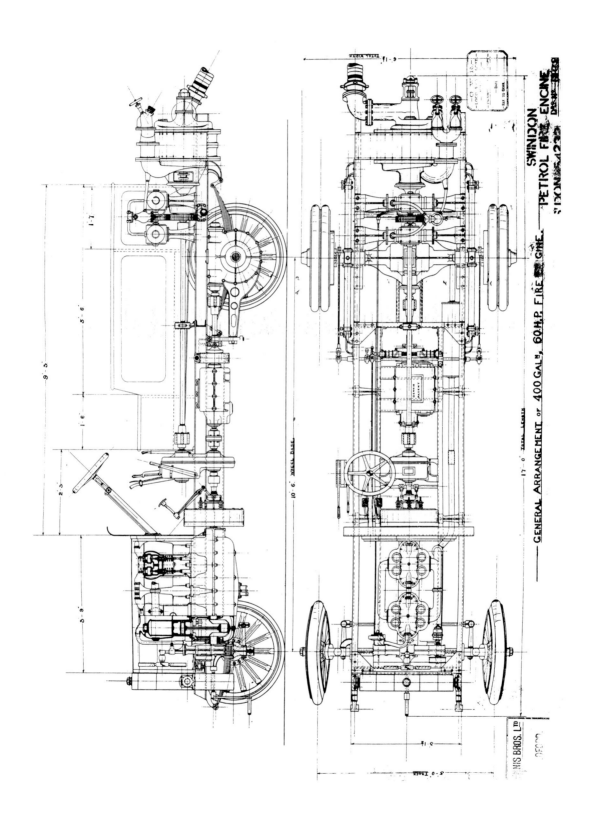

Above: General arrangement drawing of a Dennis 400-gallon 60hp fire engine.

Above: Lister Auto Trucks were built by R. A. Lister & Co Ltd of Dursley, Gloucestershire, and are seen here in use at Bristol Temple Meads Goods Depot on 2 November 1927. The fleet numbers are definitely not up to the usual signwriting standards!

Below: A Scott electric elevating platform truck on demonstration on 3 June 1947.

Left and centre left: Foden 12-ton six-wheeled rigid-framed steam wagon No S.17 is seen at Swindon Works fitted with a steam winch and condensing apparatus. The livery looks as though it could have been green with the appropriate lining. This vehicle was used on many diverse duties including manoeuvring heavy loads, such as boilers, on to low-loaders.

Below: Another unusual vehicle is this Leyland four-wheeled tractor, S1086, complete with an independent engine for towing. It is similar to the Foden steam type, but internal combustion in this case. The photograph was taken on 31 December 1937.

Above: The Great Western Railway designed and constructed a mobile motor-trailer canteen, which, when heavy air raids were experienced during World War 2, could be sent to any town on the GWR system where feeding arrangements were disorganised. Shown here at Paddington on 15 October 1941, it consisted of a four-wheeled Thornycroft tractor hauling a 6-ton Scammell drop-frame trailer with an overall length of 21 feet. The vehicle was designed at the Road Transport Department drawing office at Slough and constructed at the Carriage & Wagon Shop at Swindon.

Below: A285, a 20hp Austin limousine converted into an ambulance by the GWR, is shown here at Swindon Works on 15 January 1944, in the usual brown and cream livery. The registration number is very appropriate!

Above: No 2399, a 2-ton Morris Commercial forward-control chassis fitted with a Swindon van body, is in use as an emergency ambulance at Paddington in May 1940. The headlight is fitted with the official mask as required by World War 2 blackout regulations, and edges of the wings etc are painted white.

Below: No 233 is a Daimler limousine converted into an ambulance at Swindon Works in 1941. It appears to be painted black and looks more like a hearse! Are the door handles off condemned passenger rolling stock?

Above: Finally, credit must be given to the men without whom the Great Western Railway Road Services would not have functioned. The drivers particularly must have been a very hardy race, particularly in the very early days, without any protection at all from the weather. They also had to be mechanics, as there were very few, if any, garages along the routes. These two photographs taken in April 1915 show the type of uniform in use at that time. On the left is a motor driver, complete with breeches and gaiters, while on the right is a conductor with an ordinary suit similar to that of a railwayman. Also mention must be made of Mr F. C. A. Coventry OBE who joined the GWR in 1893. In 1902 he was appointed Assistant to the Carriage Works Manager and took charge of the Company's road motor work. He retired on 31 October 1942 in the position of Superintendent of Road Transport. The development of both cartage and passenger services on the GWR were all down to him and his staff. He really was a pioneer.

Appendices

Appendix I. 'Motor Car' Service Statistics

Copy of the Report to the Traffic Committee dated 21 January 1904.

Motor Car Services are now in operation between

		Distance
Road 1	Helston Station & Lizard	11 miles
Road 2	Penzance Station, Newlyn & Marazion	4½ miles
Road 3	Chalford & Stonehouse Stations	7 miles

Number of passengers carried to 31 December 1903

		Service Commenced	Total Passrs
1	Helston	17 August 1903	7,042
2	Penzance	31 October 1903	16,091
3	Chalford	12 October 1903	100,661

Week ending 2 January 1904 working results

Service	Tfc Receipts	Working Expenses	Car Miles Run	Receipts per mile	Working expenses per car mile
Helston	£413.13.6	£362.10.11	7,960	1s 0.48d	10.92d
Penzance	£198.19.3	£205.17.1	4,915	9.71d	10.05d
Chalford	£819.9.4	£363.8.7	14,011	1s 2.03d	6.22d

Note: for depreciation and interest £97.11.1 should be added to Helston expenses, £62.19.0 to Penzance expenses and £98.0.6 to Chalford expenses.

Appendix II. Payments to Drivers

In the early days the drivers were paid in the following manner:

1 Standing money	21s to 29s a week
2 Mileage money	2d for every 10 miles run in service
	4d for every 10 miles on Sunday.
3 Petrol bonus	1d a gallon for every gallon saved over a consumption of 4 miles a gallon (8 miles for light parcels vans)

Appendix III. Official Drawings of GWR Horse-drawn Vehicles

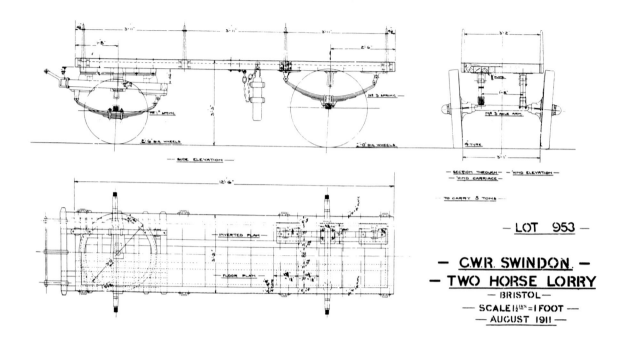

- SIDE ELEVATION -

- SECTION THROUGH -   - HIND ELEVATION -
- HIND CARRIAGE -

- TO CARRY 3 TONS -

- LOT 953 -

- G.W.R. SWINDON. -

- TWO HORSE LORRY -

- BRISTOL -

- SCALE 1½ INS = 1 FOOT -

- AUGUST 1911 -

Scale: 7mm/ft.

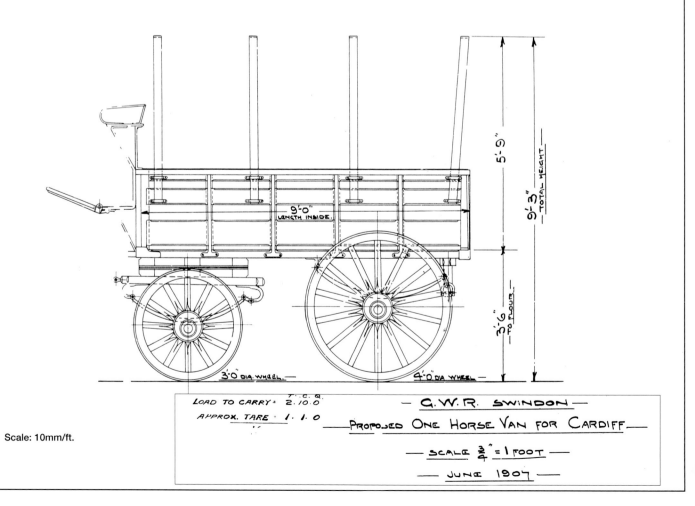

| LOAD TO CARRY = | T. C. Q. 2. 10. 0 |
| APPROX. TARE | 1. 1. 0 |

- G.W.R. SWINDON -

PROPOSED ONE HORSE VAN FOR CARDIFF

- SCALE ¾" = 1 FOOT -

- JUNE 1907 -

Scale: 10mm/ft.

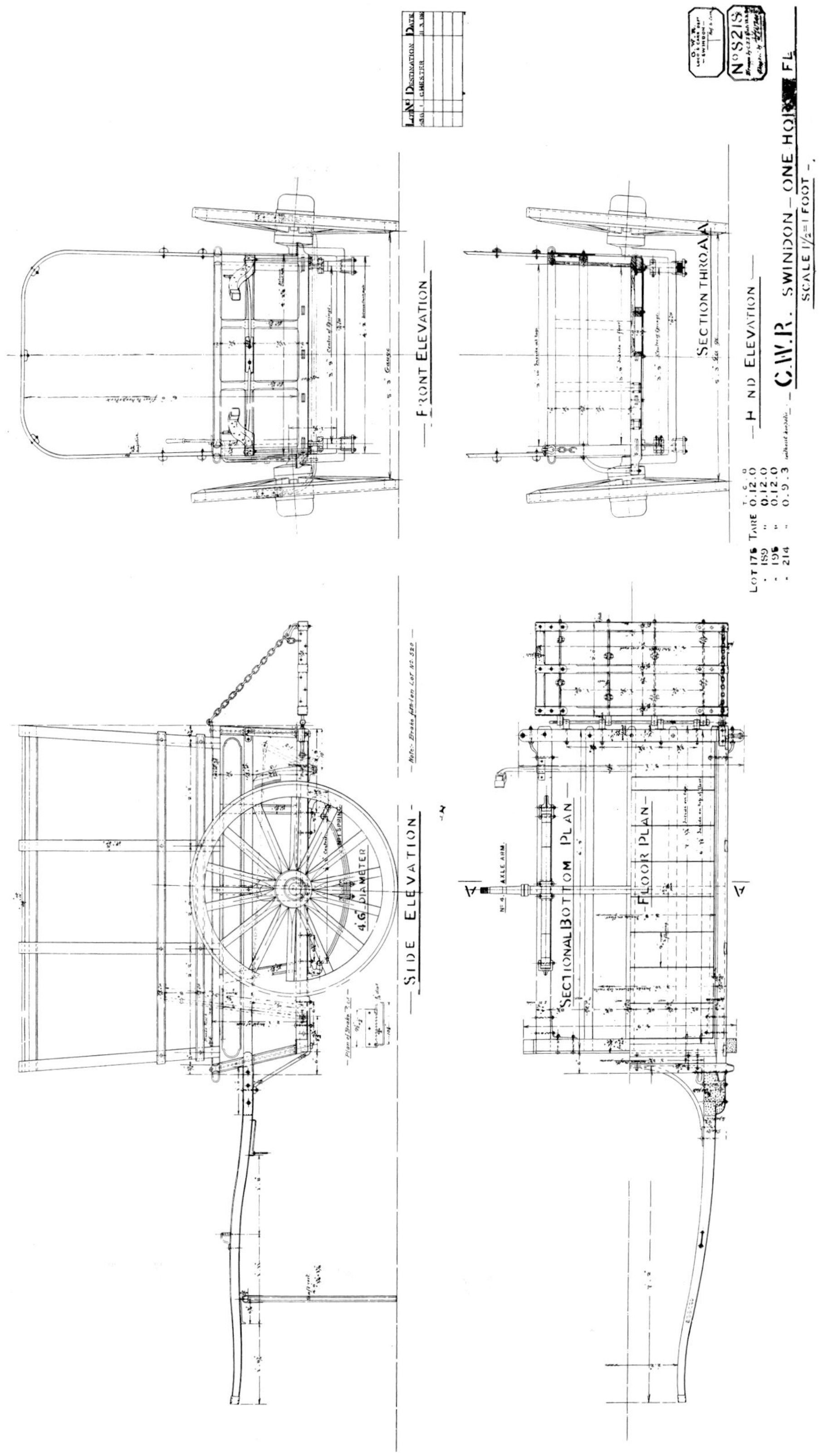

Scale: 7mm/ft.

— FRONT ELEVATION —

— SIDE ELEVATION —

— END ELEVATION —

— SECTION THROUGH A A —

— SECTIONAL BOTTOM PLAN —

— FLOOR PLAN —

4' 6" DIAMETER

G.W.R. SWINDON — ONE HORSE FL

— SCALE 1/2 = 1 FOOT —

LOT 176	TARE	T. C. Q
		0.12.0
— 189	—	0.12.0
— 196	—	0.12.0
— 214	—	0.9.3

233

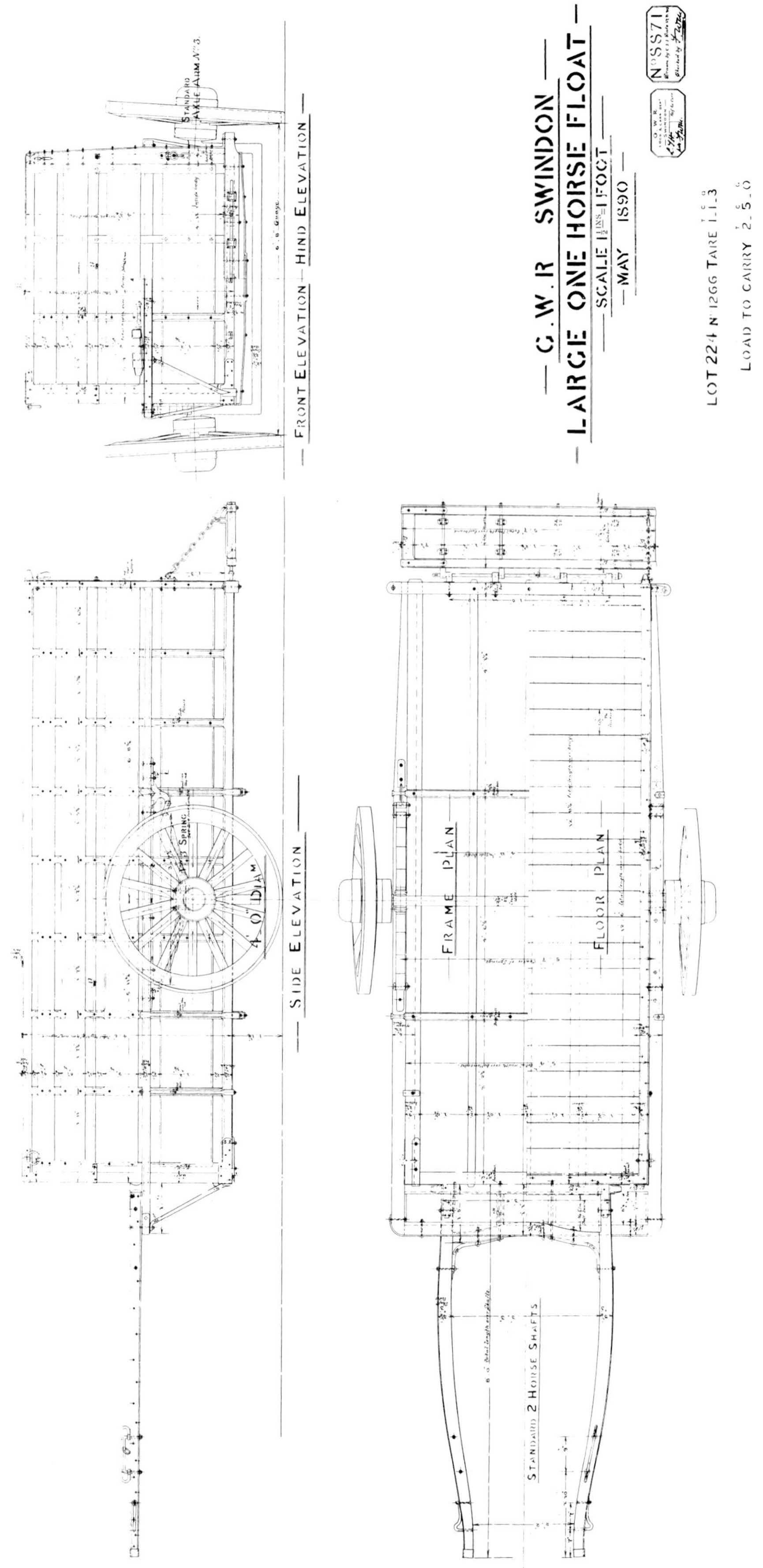

—G.W.R SWINDON—
—LARGE ONE HORSE FLOAT—
SCALE 1½INS=1FOOT
—MAY 1890—

LOT 224 N 1266 TARE 1.1.3
LOAD TO CARRY 2.5.0

FRONT ELEVATION—HIND ELEVATION

STANDARD
AXLE ALUM N°3.

SIDE ELEVATION

4. 0 DIAM

FRAME PLAN

FLOOR PLAN

STANDARD 2 HORSE SHAFTS

Scale: 7mm/ft.

Scale: 10mm/ft.

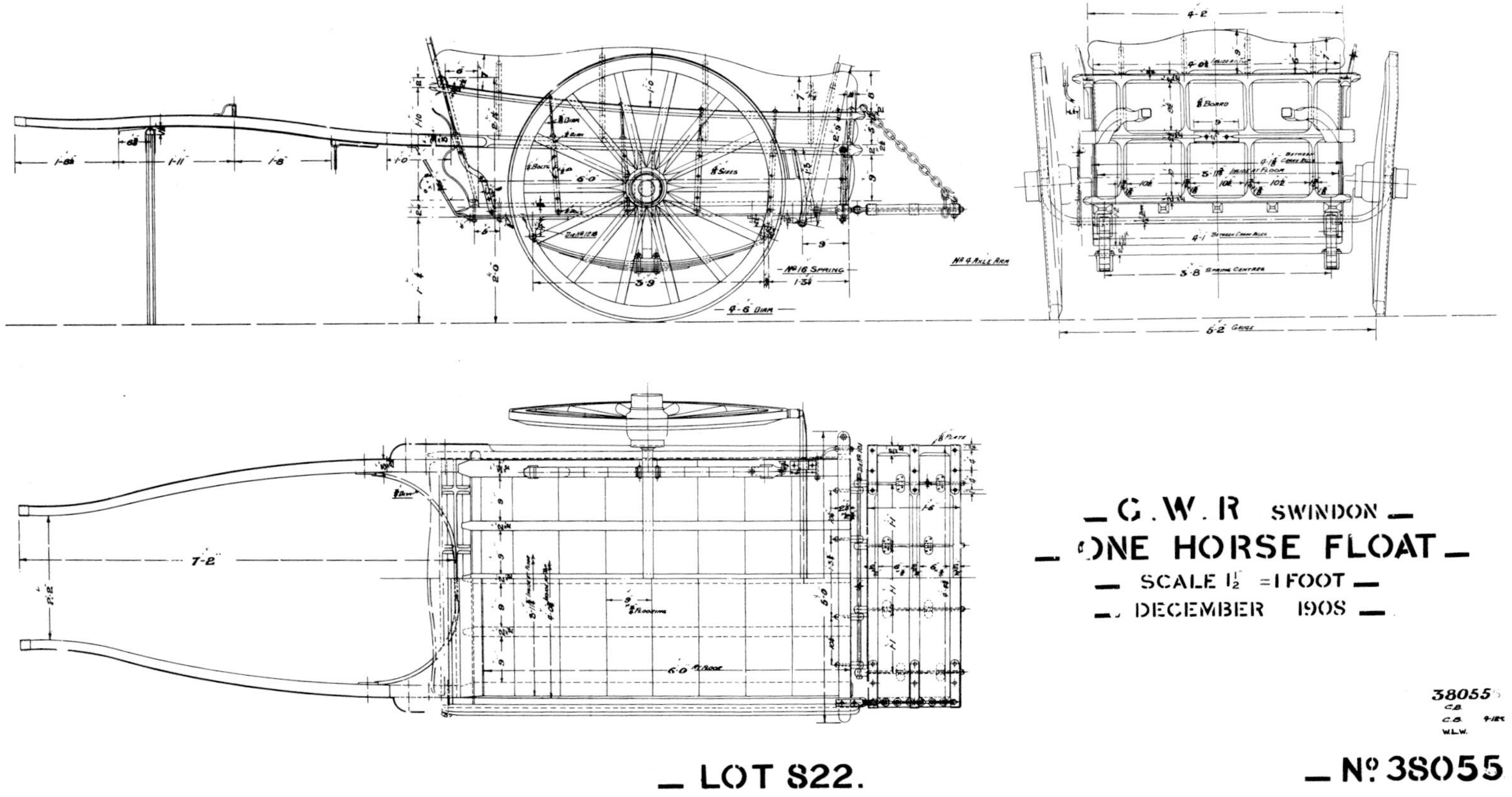

— G.W.R SWINDON —
— ONE HORSE FLOAT —
— SCALE 1½" = 1 FOOT —
— DECEMBER 1908 —
38055
C.B.
C.B.
W.L.W.
— No. 38055
— LOT 822.
No 16 SPRING
No 4 AXLE ARM
4-6 DIAM
6-2 GAUGE
3-8 SPRING CENTRES
4-2
7-2
6-0

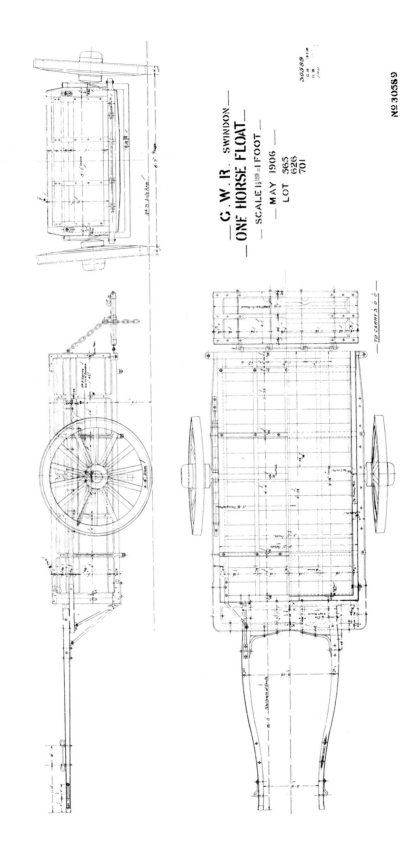

G. W. R. SWINDON
— ONE HORSE FLOAT —
SCALE 1½ INS=1 FOOT
MAY 1906
LOT 565
      626
      701

Nº 30589

Scale: 7mm/ft.

236

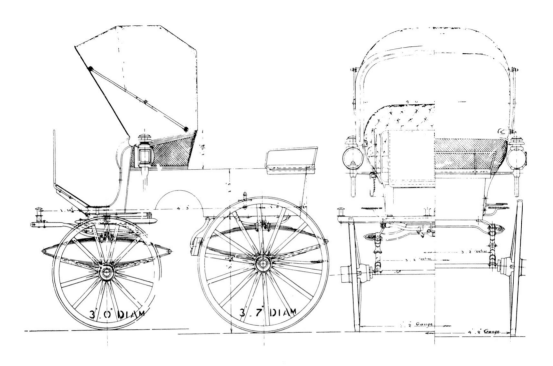

3'·0" DIAM   3'·7" DIAM

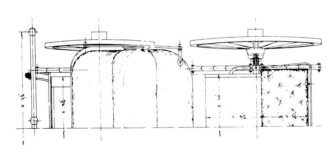

__MAIL__ __PHAETON__

__SCALE 1¼"=1FOOT__

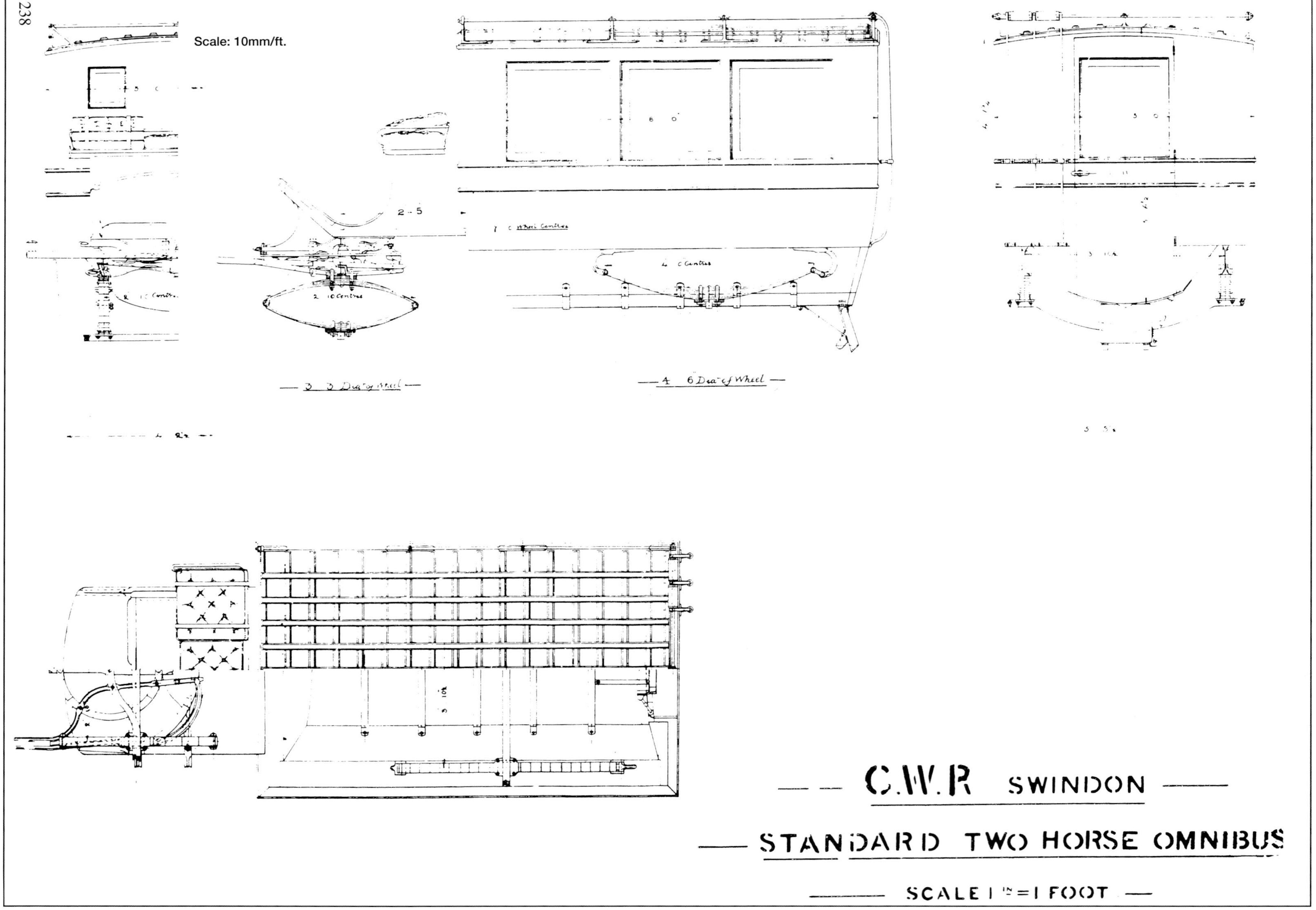

Scale: 10mm/ft.
2 - 5
2 10 Centres
4 C Centres
3 3 Dia. of Wheel
4 6 Dia. of Wheel
G.W.R SWINDON
STANDARD TWO HORSE OMNIBUS
SCALE 1 IN = 1 FOOT

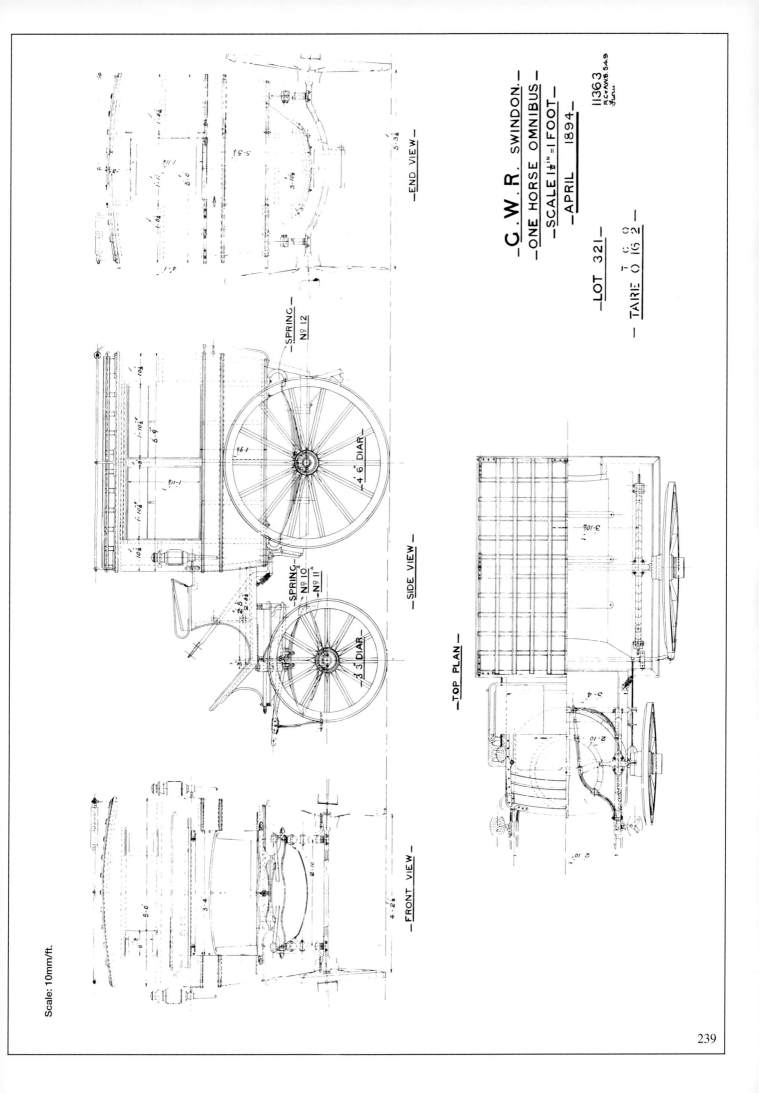

Scale: 10mm/ft.

G.W.R. SWINDON.
— ONE HORSE OMNIBUS —
— SCALE 1½ IN = 1 FOOT —
— APRIL 1894 —

11363

— LOT 321 —

— TARE 0 16 2 —

— END VIEW —

— SIDE VIEW —

SPRING Nº 12

4' 6" DIAR

SPRING Nº 10
Nº 11

3' 3" DIAR

— FRONT VIEW —

— TOP PLAN —

239

Scale: 7mm/ft.

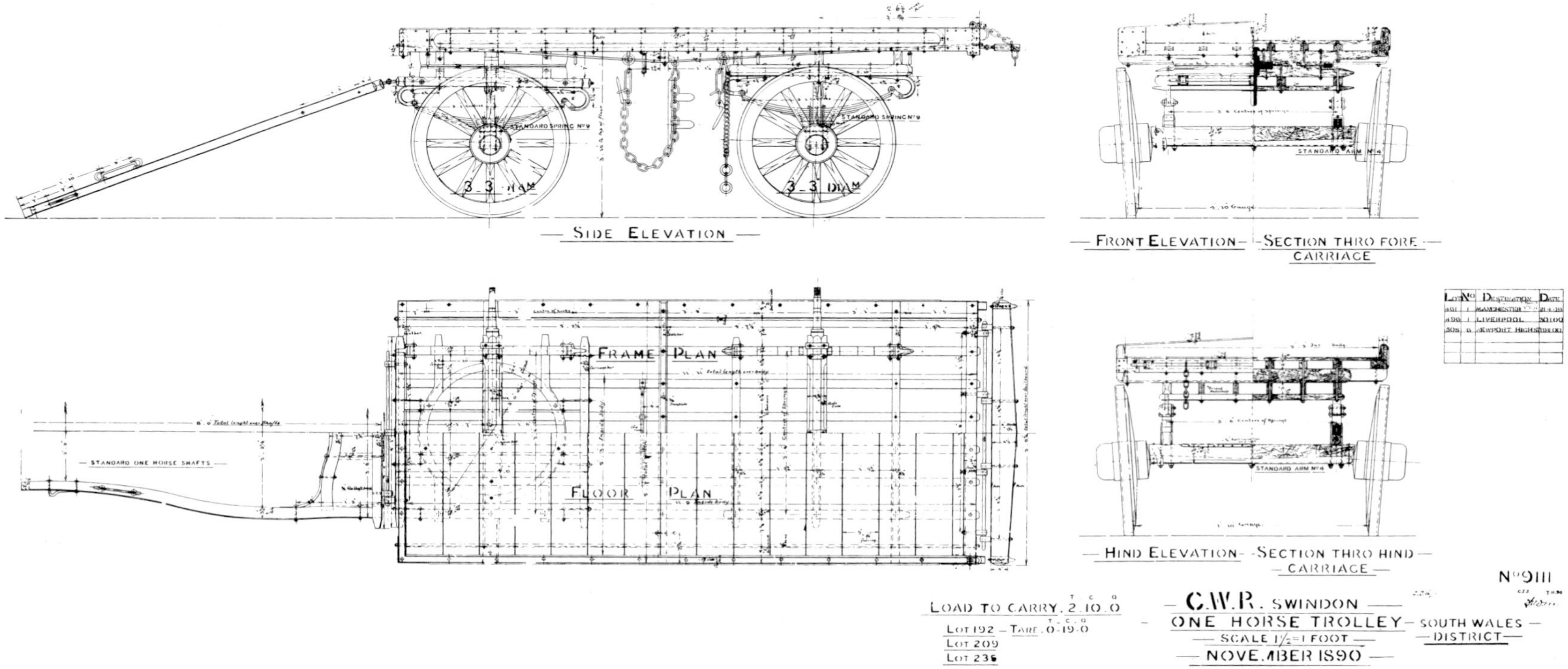
STANDARD SPRING No 9
3' 3" DIA M
SIDE ELEVATION
FRONT ELEVATION - SECTION THRO FORE CARRIAGE
STANDARD ARM No 4
FRAME PLAN
FLOOR PLAN
STANDARD ONE HORSE SHAFTS
HIND ELEVATION - SECTION THRO HIND CARRIAGE
No 9111
LOAD TO CARRY. 2.10.0
LOT 192 - TARE. 0.19.0
LOT 209
LOT 236
G.W.R. SWINDON
ONE HORSE TROLLEY - SOUTH WALES DISTRICT
SCALE 1½ = 1 FOOT
NOVEMBER 1890

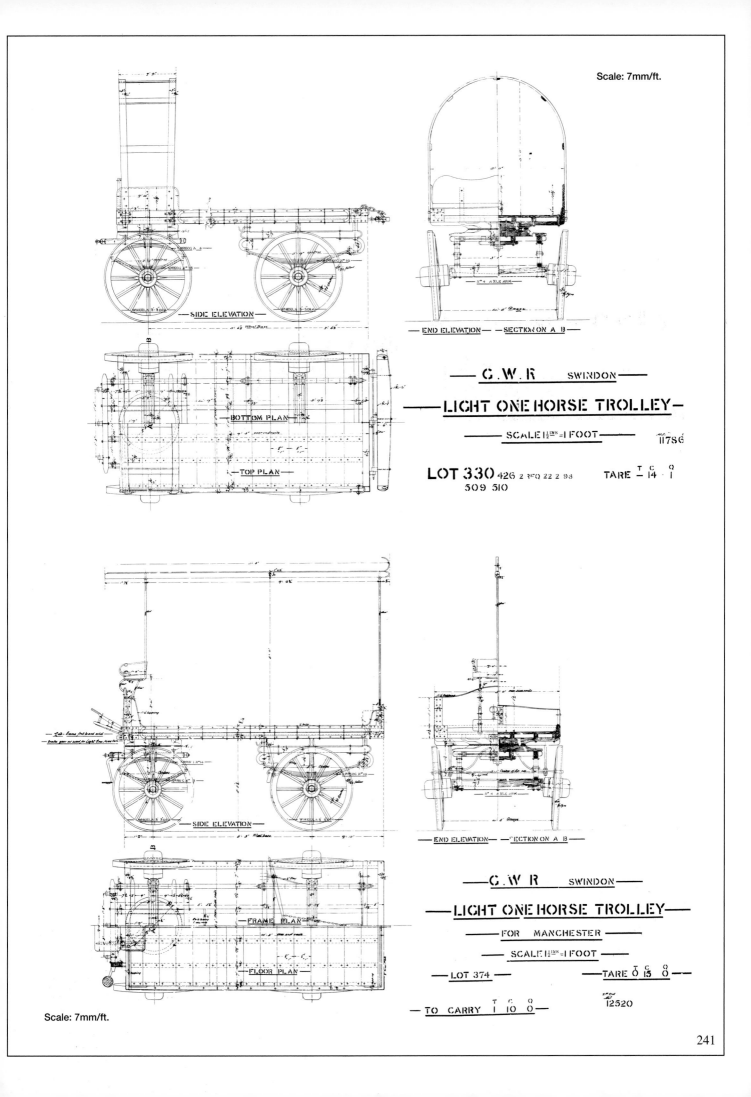

Scale: 7mm/ft.

— SIDE ELEVATION —

BOTTOM PLAN

TOP PLAN

— END ELEVATION — SECTION ON A B —

— G.W.R   SWINDON —

—LIGHT ONE HORSE TROLLEY—

— SCALE 1½ INS =1 FOOT —   11786

LOT 330 426 2 RFQ 22 2 98   TARE T C Q 14 1
509 510

— SIDE ELEVATION —

FRAME PLAN

FLOOR PLAN

— END ELEVATION — SECTION ON A B —

— G.W R   SWINDON —

—LIGHT ONE HORSE TROLLEY—

— FOR MANCHESTER —

— SCALE 1½ INS =1 FOOT —

— LOT 374 —   TARE T C Q 0 15 0

12520

— TO CARRY T C Q 1 10 0 —

Scale: 7mm/ft.

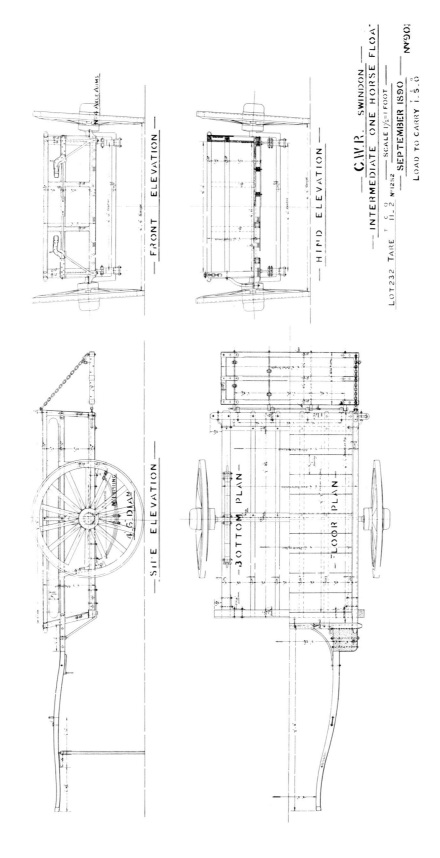

— FRONT ELEVATION —

— HIND ELEVATION —

— SIDE ELEVATION —

— BOTTOM PLAN —

— FLOOR PLAN —

4.6 DIAM

G.W.R. SWINDON
— INTERMEDIATE ONE HORSE FLOAT —
SCALE 1/2 = 1 FOOT
LOT 232 TARE T. C. Q. Nº 1282
11 - 2
SEPTEMBER 1890
Nº 901
LOAD TO CARRY 1 - 5 - 0

Scale: 7mm/ft.

242

Scale: 10mm/ft.

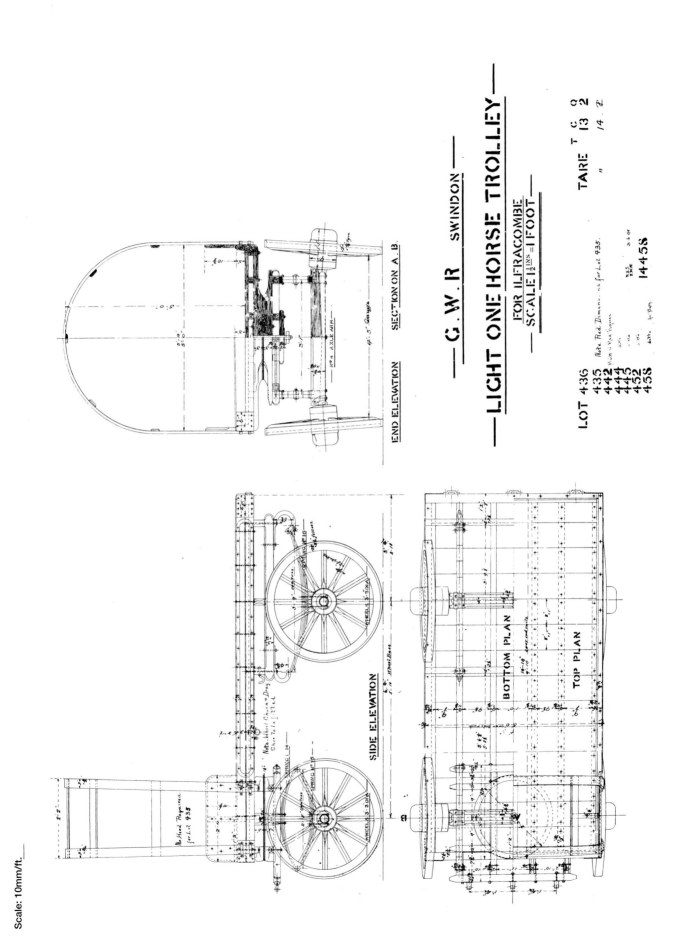

— G. W. R SWINDON —

— LIGHT ONE HORSE TROLLEY —

FOR ILFRACOMBE
SCALE 1½ INS = 1 FOOT

END ELEVATION

SECTION ON A. B.

SIDE ELEVATION

BOTTOM PLAN

TOP PLAN

TARE

	T	C	Q
	13	2	0
"	14		2

LOT 436
435
442
444
445
452
458

14458

243

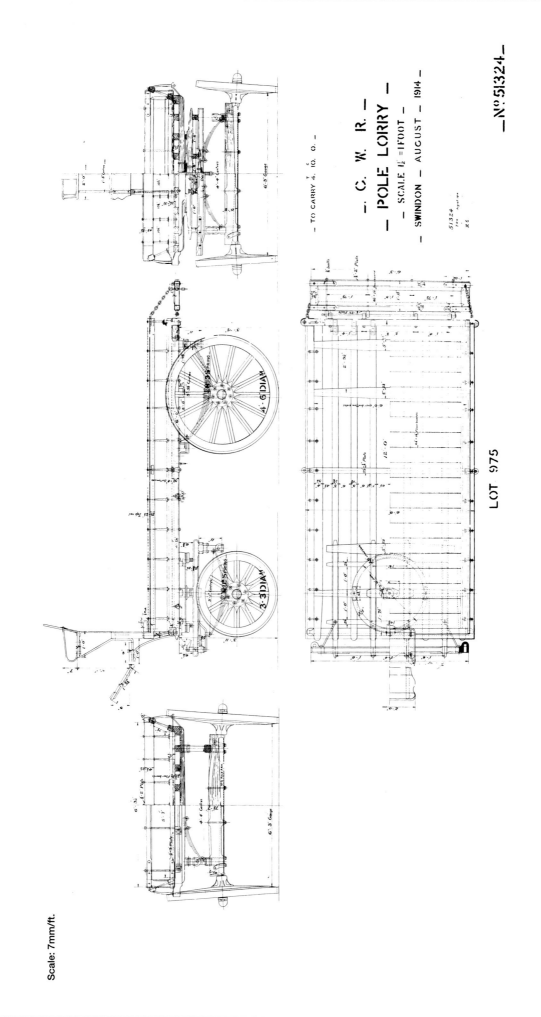

– C. W. R. –
– POLE LORRY –
– SCALE 1½" = 1 FOOT –
– SWINDON – AUGUST – 1914 –

– TO CARRY 4. 10. 0. –

– Nº 51324 –

LOT 975

Scale: 7mm/ft.

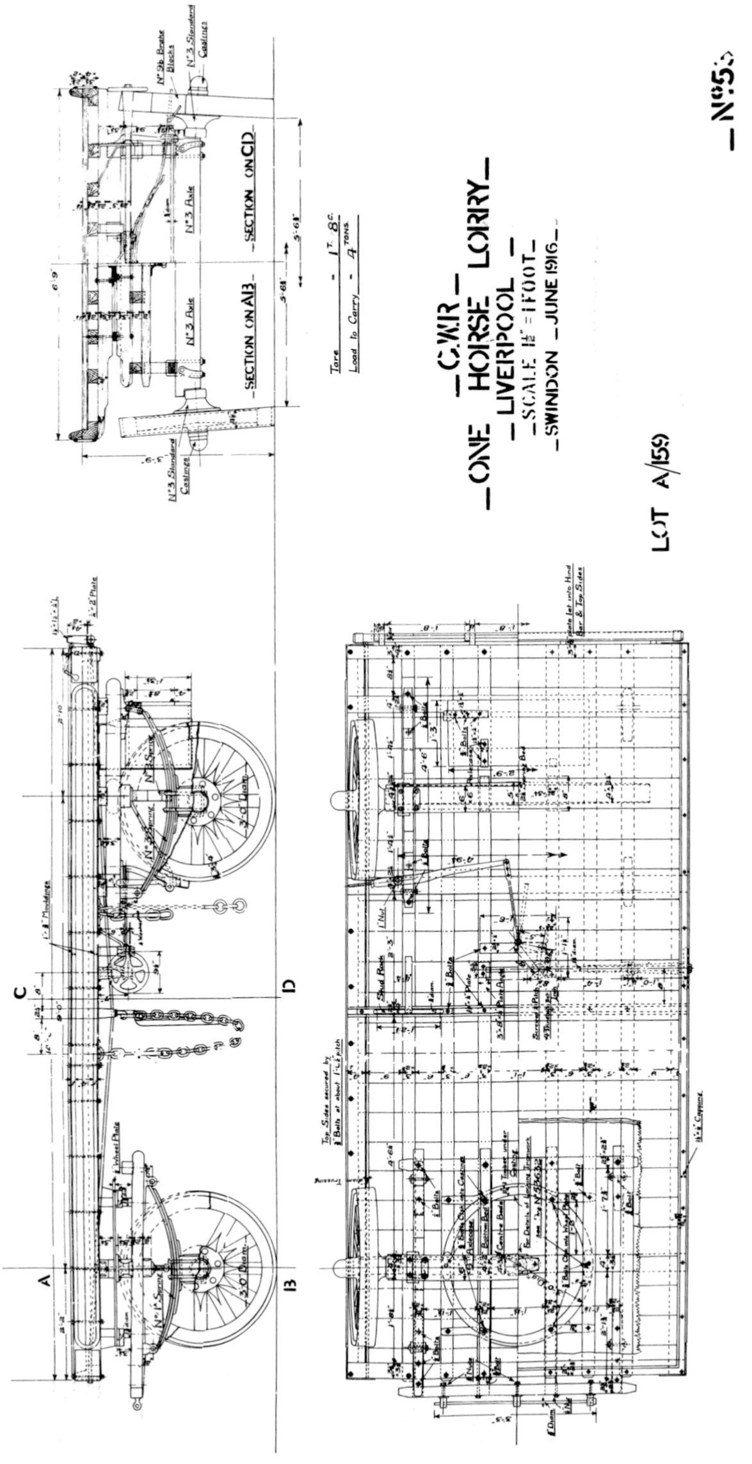

Scale: 7mm/ft.

GWR
ONE HORSE LORRY
LIVERPOOL
SCALE 1½" = 1 FOOT
SWINDON JUNE 1916

Tare 1 T. 8 C.
Load to Carry 4 Tons

LOT A/159

SECTION ON AB   SECTION ON CD

No 5.

Scale: 7mm/ft.

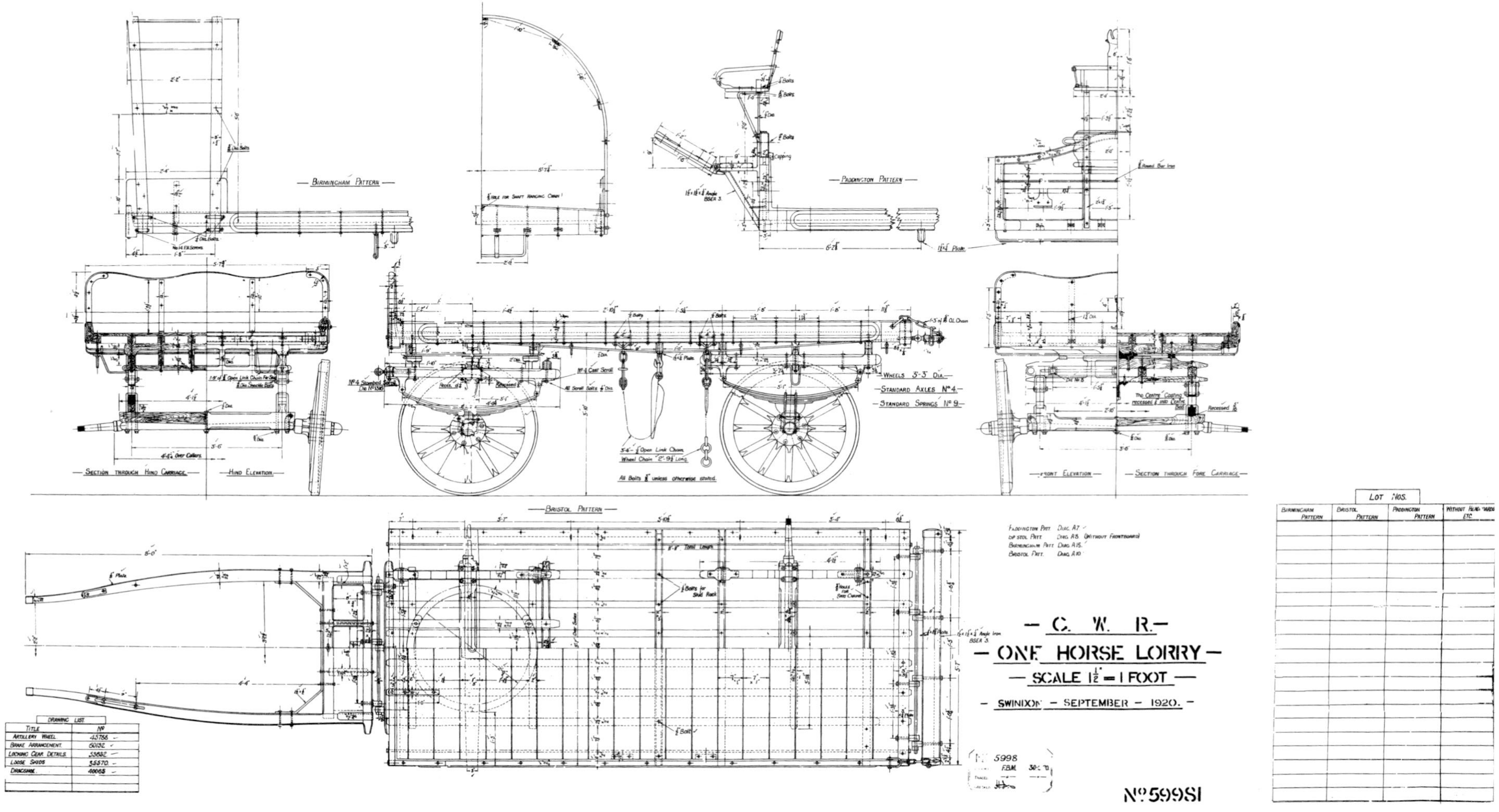

Birmingham Pattern
Paddington Pattern
Bristol Pattern
Section through Hind Carriage
Hind Elevation
Front Elevation
Section through Fore Carriage
Wheels 5'-3" Dia.
Standard Axles Nº 4.
Standard Springs Nº 9.
All Bolts ⅝" unless otherwise stated.
Lot Nos.
Birmingham Pattern
Bristol Pattern
Paddington Pattern
Without Head-board etc.
Drawing List
Title
Nº
Artillery Wheel
45788
Brake Arrangement
60132
Locking Gear Details
55692
Loose Skids
55570
Drag Shoe
40065
Paddington Patt. Diag. A7
Bristol Patt. Diag. A8 (without Frontboard)
Birmingham Patt. Diag. A15.
Bristol Patt. Diag. A10.
— G. W. R. —
— ONE HORSE LORRY —
— SCALE 1½" = 1 FOOT —
— SWINDON — SEPTEMBER — 1920. —
5998
F.B.M.
Nº 59981

Scale: 7mm/ft.

HIND ELEVATION — SECTION THRO HIND CARRIAGE

SIDE ELEVATION

FRONT ELEVATION — SECTION THRO FORE CARRIAGE

3.3 DIAM

3.3.DIAM

BOTTOM PLAN

FLOOR PLAN

For Details of Drawing
Fore Carriage Springs	No 2514
Hind Carriage Springs	No 2514
Hind Carr Ironwork	No 2514
Wheels Fore & Hind	No 4645
Axle Arms	No 4670

C.W.R. — SWINDON
TWO HORSE TROLLEY
SCALE 1½=1 FOOT
DECEMBER 1889

Lot 182 & 193. Tare 1.7.3
405
307

LOAD TO CARRY 4.10.0

Nº 6551

FRONT ELEVATION—HIND ELEVATION

SIDE ELEVATION

PLAN

C.W.R. SWINDON

LOT #07 #73

4½ TON TIMBER CARRIAGE

SCALE 1¾ INS = 1 FOOT

MAY 1891

LOT 162
TARE Nº 1202
Nº 1204

T.C.Q
1.5.1
1.6.3

LOAD TO CARRY 4.10.0

Scale: 7mm/ft.

248

Scale: 7mm/ft.

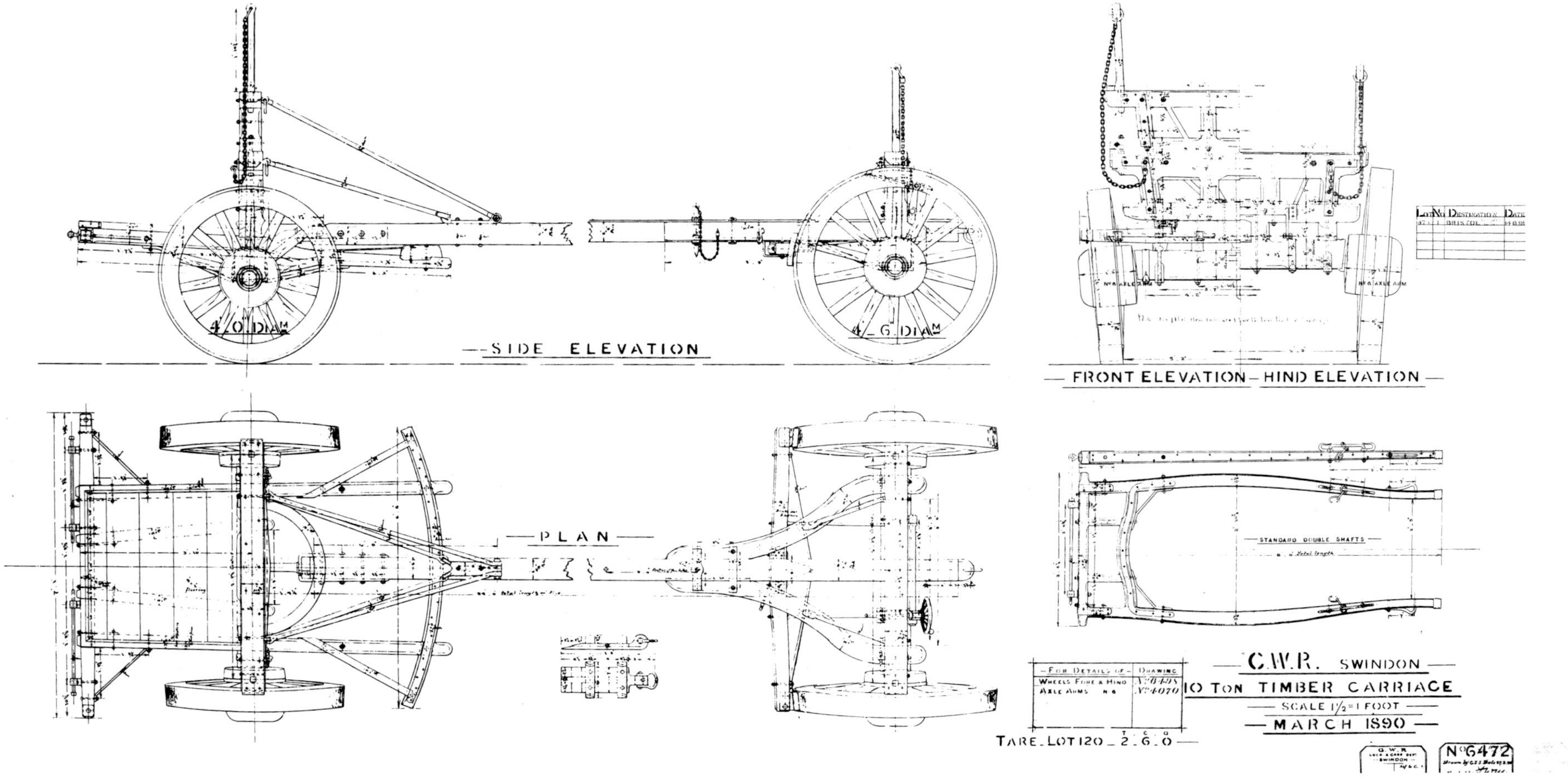

FRONT ELEVATION – HIND ELEVATION

G.W.R. SWINDON
10 TON TIMBER CARRIAGE
SCALE 1/2 = 1 FOOT
MARCH 1890

N° 6472

STANDARD DOUBLE SHAFTS

FOR DETAILS OF	Drawing
Wheels Front & Hind	N° 4672
Axle Arms N° 6	N° 4070

TARE. LOT 120 – 2·6·0

6" DIAM

4" DIAM

SIDE ELEVATION

PLAN

249

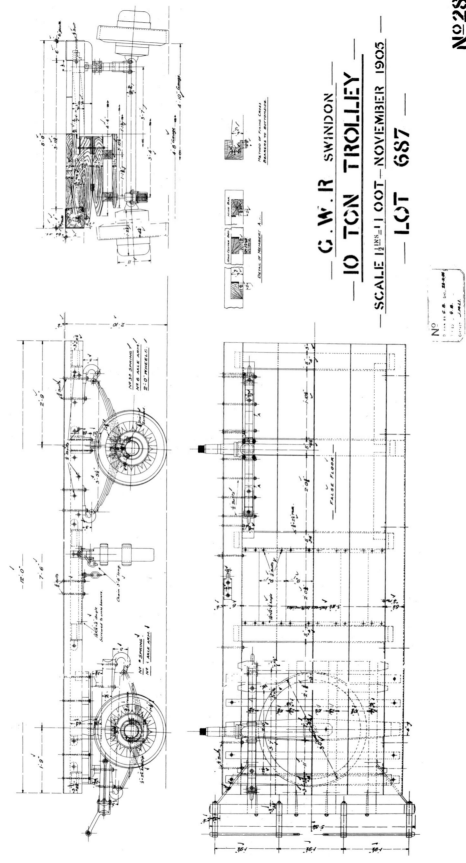

Nº 28171ᴬ

G.W.R SWINDON
10 TON TROLLEY
— SCALE 1½ᴵᴺˢ=1 OOT — NOVEMBER 1905 —
— LOT 687 —

METHOD OF FIXING CROSS
BEARERS TO BUFFERPLANK

DETAIL OF MEMBER 'A'

FALSE FLOOR

Scale: 10mm/ft.

250

Scale: 7mm/ft.

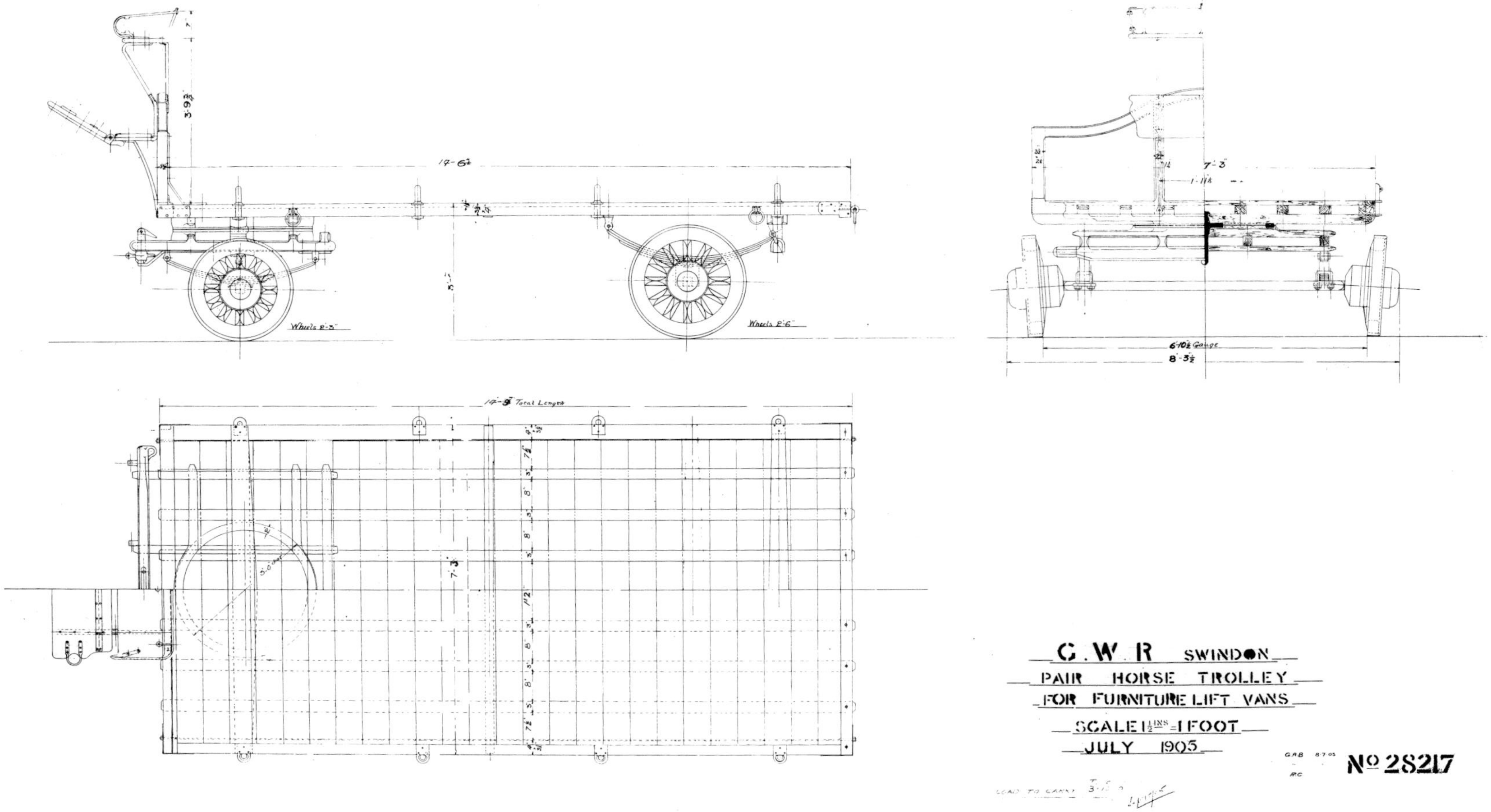

G.W.R SWINDON
PAIR HORSE TROLLEY
FOR FURNITURE LIFT VANS
SCALE 1½ LINS = 1 FOOT
JULY 1905
Nº 28217
17-6½
14-9 Total Length
Wheels 8-3
Wheels 8-6
6'10½ Gauge
8'-5½
7-3

C. W. R.
— 2 HORSE PLATE CLASS FLOAT. —
— SCALE 1½ INS. = 1 FOOT. —
— SWINDON. — SEPTEMBER. — 1921. —

No 61719

— C. W. R. —

— 4'-10" FLOAT FOR HAULAGE BY HORSE OR TRACTOR —

— SCALE 1½" = 1 FOOT —
— SWINDON — MARCH, 1931 — — Nº 94256 —

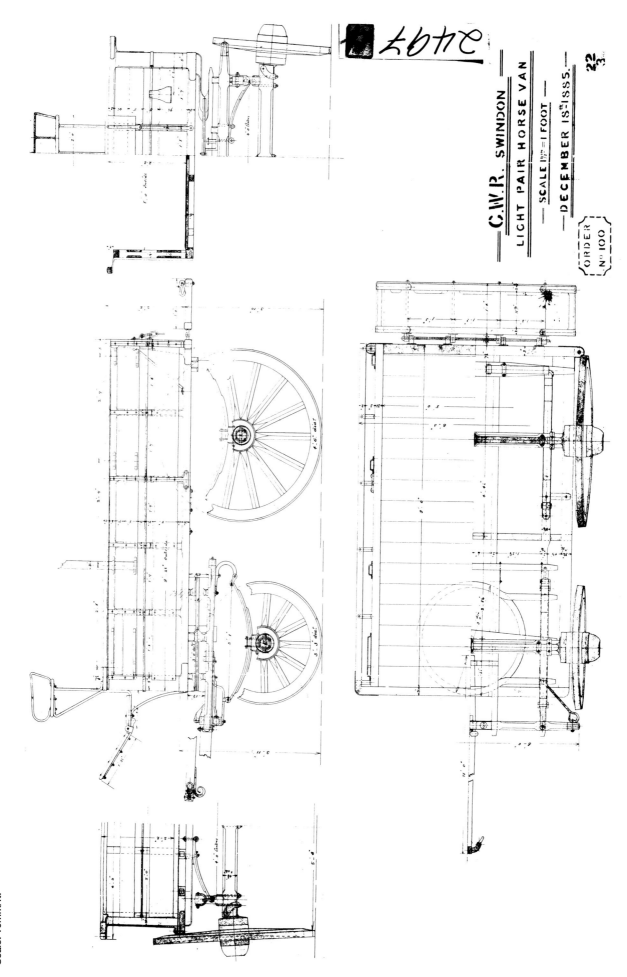

G.W.R. SWINDON

LIGHT PAIR HORSE VAN

SCALE 1½" = 1 FOOT

DECEMBER 18th 1885.

ORDER Nº 100

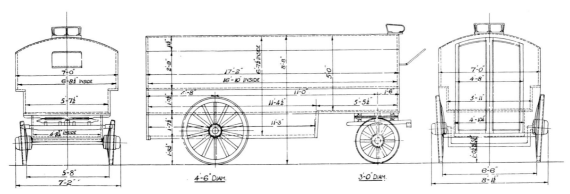

Scale: 4mm/ft.

TARE WEIGHT = 2 - 2 - 3.

G.W.R.
TWO HORSE FURNITURE VAN
Nº 2079
SCALE ½ = 1 FOOT
SWINDON   FEBRUARY 1926

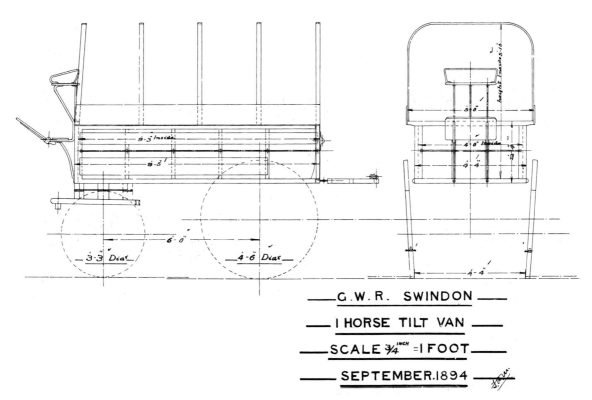

Scale: 7mm/ft.

G.W.R. SWINDON
1 HORSE TILT VAN
SCALE ¾ INCH = 1 FOOT
SEPTEMBER. 1894

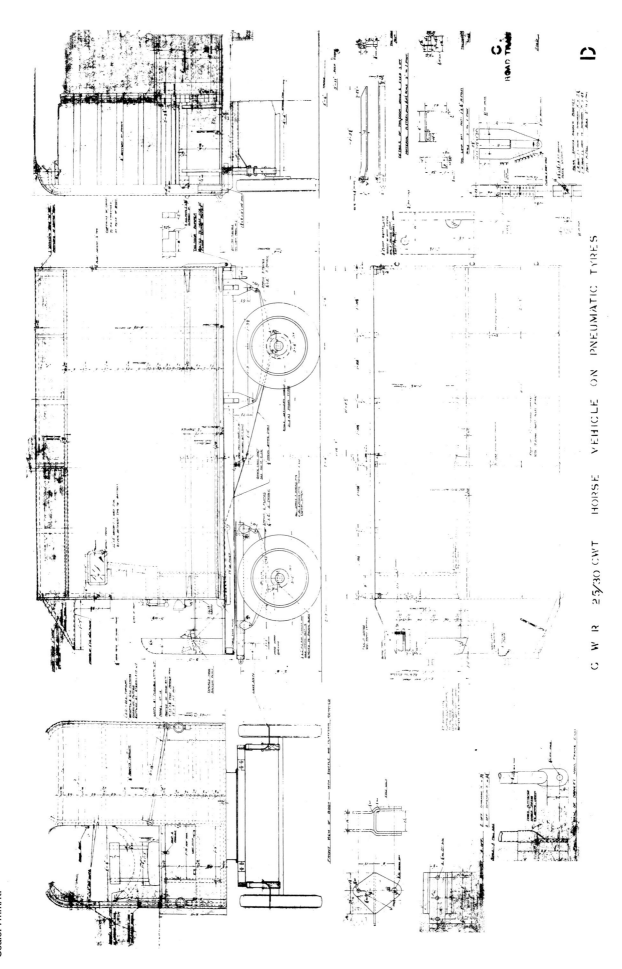

Scale: 7mm/ft.

G W R 25/30 CWT HORSE VEHICLE ON PNEUMATIC TYRES

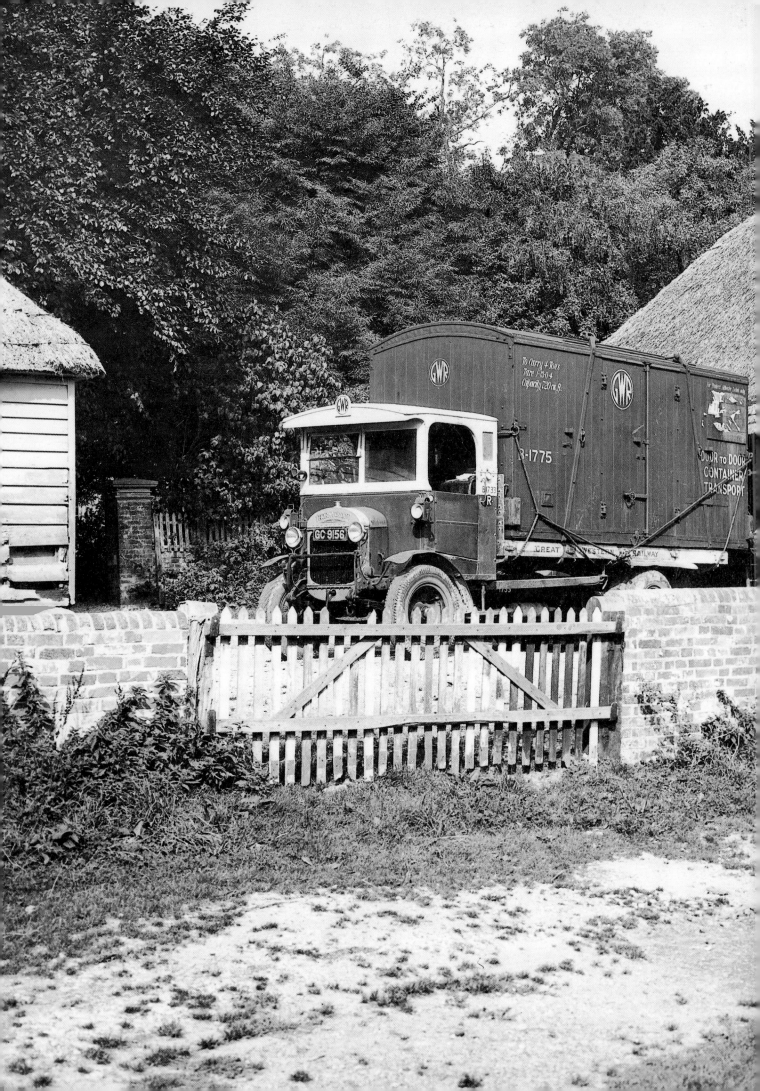